Praise for *The Creation of the Night Sky*

"A haunting multifaceted work filled with astonishing, surreal images."
                                        —*The New York Times Book Review*

Praise for *In the Year of the Comet*

"Nicholas Christopher's poems are vibrant with light and the surprise of recognition. He shows us again and again the luminous nature of the familiar."   —W. S. Merwin

"Everything here is luminous with accuracy of sight and delicacy of insight. He must now rank among the very best poets of his generation."   —Anthony Hecht

Praise for *Desperate Characters*

"By far the most gifted and inspiring new poet I have read in the past fifteen years."   —Jim Carroll

Praise for 5°

"5° deserves a place next to T. S. Eliot's *The Waste Land*."
                                        —*San Francisco Review of Books*

"I have read 5° with great pleasure and a sense of wonder . . . The book is an authentic addition to American poetry."
                                        —Harold Bloom

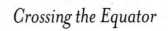

Crossing the Equator

Books by Nicholas Christopher

POETRY

Crossing the Equator: New and Selected Poems, 1972–2004
Atomic Field: Two Poems (2000)
The Creation of the Night Sky (1998)
5° (1995)
In the Year of the Comet (1992)
Desperate Characters: A Novella in Verse (1988)
A Short History of the Island of Butterflies (1986)
On Tour With Rita (1982)

FICTION

The Bestiary (2007)
Franklin Flyer (2002)
A Trip to the Stars (2000)
Veronica (1996)
The Soloist (1986)

NONFICTION

Somewhere in the Night: Film Noir & the American City (1997)

EDITOR

Walk on the Wild Side: Urban American Poetry Since 1975 (1994)
Under 35: The New Generation of American Poets (1989)

Crossing the Equator

New and Selected Poems
1972–2004

NICHOLAS
CHRISTOPHER

A HARVEST BOOK
HARCOURT, INC.

Orlando · Austin · New York · San Diego · Toronto · London

for Constance

www.HarcourtBooks.com

The Library of Congress has cataloged the hardcover edition as follows:
Christopher, Nicholas.
Crossing the Equator: new & selected poems, 1972–2004/Nicholas
Christopher.—1st ed.
p.   cm.
ISBN 978-0-15-101095-0   ISBN 978-0-15-603140-0 (pbk.)
I. Title.
PS3553.H754C76 2004
811'.54—dc22   2003024627

Text set in Mrs Eaves
Designed by Scott Piehl

Printed in the United States of America

First Harvest edition 2007
A C E G I K J H F D B

Contents

From THE CREATION OF THE NIGHT SKY (1998)

From ATOMIC FIELD: TWO POEMS (2000)

Permissions Acknowledgments

Poems from the following previously published books
are included in the present volume:

On Tour with Rita, copyright © 1982
by Nicholas Christopher; published by Alfred A. Knopf

A Short History of the Island of Butterflies, copyright © 1986
by Nicholas Christopher; published by Viking Penguin

Desperate Characters: A Novella in Verse & Other Poems, copyright © 1988
by Nicholas Christopher; published by Viking Penguin

In the Year of the Comet, copyright © 1992
by Nicholas Christopher; published by Viking Penguin

5° & Other Poems, copyright © 1995
by Nicholas Christopher; published by Penguin Books

The Creation of the Night Sky, copyright © 1998
by Nicholas Christopher; published by Harcourt Brace

Atomic Field: Two Poems, copyright © 2000
by Nicholas Christopher; published by Harcourt

These poems first appeared in *The New Yorker:*

"Double Solitaire," "Heat," "Walt Whitman at the Reburial of
Poe," "Nocturne for Miranda," "The Track," "On the Meridian,"
"Rimbaud Crossing the Alps," "The Public Gardens," "Evening,"
"Leaving Town," "The House Where Lord Rochester Died,"
"Winter Night," "Cardiac Arrest," "Losing Altitude," "Musical
Chairs," "Krazy Kat," "Green Animals," "Outside Perpignan in
Heavy Rain," "In the Country," "On the Peninsula," "Reading
the Sunday Comics, Summer 1963," "Mrs. Luna,"
"Midsummer," "1972:3"

Some of the new poems were originally published in the following:

The New Yorker: "The Last Hours of Laódikê,
Sister of Hektor," "Lake Como"

The New York Times Book Review: "Trópico"

The Paris Review: "Ultima Thule" and "Robert Desnos
in Havana, 1928"

NEW POEMS

Lake Como

The searchlight of a February moon
at the end of the street

bare trees black railing
an eastern star set like a pearl atop a steeple

that shadows the doorway
where the one-armed card sharp squats

shuffling his deck on a milk crate
waiting for the No. 6 bus to discharge

the off-duty cop the seamstress
the drunken mechanic and the clerk on crutches

who pauses before his building to watch
the mechanic lose three dollars at blackjack

and then stiffly ascends the five flights
to his two rooms on a shaftway

hanging his coat on a hook
and sitting down at the table

on which this morning he placed
a soup bowl and spoon

a tin of crackers and the crossword
puzzle he had been laboring over

beneath the gaze of his late wife
her color photograph propped up in a small frame

a young woman in a boxy dress and felt cap
waving shyly by the edge of a lake

where over her shoulder beneath a clear sky
a sailboat rides the wind

passengers on the polished deck
gazing at the glowing mountain peaks

the cypresses lining the shore
and the pink palazzi with ancient gardens

these men and women in white
who seem to live upon the water

gliding among themselves oblivious to strife
and all else that wears a body down

some sipping from crystal goblets
others just drinking in the light

The Last Hours of Laódikê, Sister of Hektor
(a poem of September 11)

Cold missiles and a rain
of embers accompany the men
who slide like shadows into the city
faces mud-smeared
stones for teeth no eyes

who slit the throats of everyone
they encounter until breaking down
my door they drag me into the darkness
that floods the corridor
and lock me in an icy chamber

where a torch of thorns sputters
and a man more bone than flesh
is playing music old
as time itself on a flute
and a girl clutching her knees

burns with fever before I apply
a square of moonlight to her brow
before she whispers her name
my name
both of us falling now

the room falling too and the city
and no one to hear our cries
just the dead waiting in a bottomless canyon
and the sound relentless
of the gods grinding this world to dust

Trópico

On the abandoned tennis court in the coconut grove
where the cows chew weeds along the baseline

and a halved ball like a temple's dome shadows
an anthill of powdered clay to which a column

of red ants marches out of the grass
lugging bread crumbs from a ditchdigger's

lunch scavenged by the roadside
and grape seeds spat out a truck window

by a girl with windblown hair returning barefoot
from a dance the previous night

and finally a fly's carcass minus the wing
that a straggler ant is struggling to carry

when a gecko slithers from the weeds to snap him up
before being snatched away himself hours later

asleep behind transparent eyelids on a fallen
palm by a trembler a nocturnal bird

whose plumage sparkles with stars as he flies
over the road where a truck is speeding

with no girl inside tonight to taste the wind
and drawing in his wings dives into the forest

a black curtain he pierces like a needle
allowing a pinpoint of light to escape

14 rue Serpentine

a Paris Notebook

I.

On the arched ceiling
of the attic guest room
a visitor once painted a sky so real
(clouds lit from within
sailing against a brilliant blue)
that others have awakened beneath it
believing they were lying
in an alpine meadow
a stream rushing by and breezes
laced with pollen brushing their cheeks
Who was this visitor you ask
when did he come here
and when did he leave

2.

In the Egyptian Gallery at the Louvre you wonder:
if the priests of the XIIth Dynasty were correct
and our dreams are memories of past lives
shattered and rearranged by the gods
if the truth is camouflaged
in the token correspondences of this world
names dates places that can be linked with ease
by even a minor deity
then the inscrutable mysteries which have tormented
you and your tormentors ought to come clear
so simple suddenly:
Happiness awaits all of us
but few find their way to her

3.

You're dreaming of the velodrome
the rings of Saturn spinning
with riders who blur away
like those fast-motion films
of flowers blossoming and dying
or of the moon in a roiled sky
sailing through its phases
Tonight the moon rises above rooftops & bridges
spreading its sea of silver light
stilling vast crowds
and for an instant reflected whole
in the spectacles of a blind man
sitting alone in a parked car

4.

The owl no bigger than your fist
speckled blue and black
is still hooting at dawn in the courtyard
when you open a letter from a friend
grieving for his daughter
quoting Martial who mourned the death
of another child twenty centuries ago
Earth, lie not heavy on her who walked so lightly on you
Sometimes it's not hours but years that pass in a single day
and when darkness falls again
drawing you into its circle
will you hear that same owl
or will another be perched in its place?

5.

In the back room where a ray of light
has penetrated the vine-covered window
the green curtain that parts
onto the circular garden
you dip your hands into a basin of water
and they blur away
only the lines from your upturned palms remain
floating for an instant
rearranging themselves
a map etched in disappearing ink
to guide you for the rest of your life
or until you leave this address
whichever comes first

6.

On the kitchen table
a pot of bitter tea steeps
beside a bowl of dates
a plate of toast with white honey
coconut milk in a pitcher
and the jade statue of the goddess
with twelve arms brandishing swords
and sixty fingernails painted gold
her head thrown back in laughter
In a single battle
how many men could she slay
in a single night
how many embrace

7.

Tattooed on your shoulder
the likeness of a fish
with golden scales silver fins
and a single ruby eye
a creature last seen three millennia ago
near the Nile delta
reputed to have entrails of pearls
coveted by the fishermen who lined
the riverbank for miles
and waded into the reeds
shoulder to shoulder netting the fish
and gutting it for treasure not flesh
until it was rendered extinct

8.

At dusk rain slants in from the north
black needles clotting
the locomotive's cyclops beam
the prison searchlight
the street lamp's cone
beneath which vagrants line their boots
with road maps before closing their eyes
and entering a maze of blind alleys
searching for the one doorway among thousands
that will lead away from their nightmares
and the one in a million
(where the rain dissolves into light)
that opens onto paradise

9.

The snake charmer's daughter
born in a carnival tent
with a crescent of stars on her brow
has opened a storefront studio next door
The Serpent Priestess she calls herself
bracelets jangling while she arranges
tarot cards on a zodiac wheel
explaining that this street was named
not for its windingness but for the snakes
Napoleon's soldiers brought back from Egypt
which infest the neighborhood
though you yourself have only seen one:
the cobra coiled in a basket at her feet

10.

Dip your rotting oars
into the brown waters of the lake
and row toward the floating temple
Splinters of light escape its shuttered windows
a red lantern sways on the dock
a candle flutters by the door
You can hear the faintest sound:
fruit falling in the orchard
a snake shedding its skin in the reeds
Your breathing too is shallow
your hands are one with the darkness
and you know when you reach the temple
your oars will be gone

II.

A friend of a friend chops and sautées
morel mushrooms leeks and celery root
punctuating the narrative of her life's journey
with Sufi epigrams such as
The candle is not there to illuminate itself
Deft with a knife and light on her feet
she decants a sauterne and declares
that she only cooks for strangers
food unlike love tenderness or true passion
so easy to give so readily received
For most men she says the more elaborate
the meal the greater the illusion of fulfillment whereas
If you are entertaining a dervish, dry bread is enough

12.

You cross the hall with an empty glass
and return with it empty again
passing a mirror that remains blank
a birdcage with an open door
and an orrery of the solar system
the planets their moons and even a famous comet
all of them orbiting a wooden sun painted gold
The water you just drank was so cold
it could have been drawn from the iceberg
the size of Delaware
that recently broke away from Antarctica—
your destination perhaps a small voice whispers
the next time you get out of bed

13.

What is the music that breaks into your sleep
leaving you to shiver beside the stove
with a single lingering image
the bridge in the Venetian lagoon
connecting Burano and Mazzorbo
that you crossed in a storm
a bridge identical to the one a psychic drew
for you in a nightclub in Prague
spanning (she said) the twin shores
of birth and death
their reefs invisible to all men
their deep currents liable to divert you
for an eternity

14.

So the dead are among us again
even here where Halloween is not celebrated
and the moon flies through the skeletons of trees
and men in rowboats fish for souls on the river
There is a woman with spidery hair swinging a lantern
disappearing down the colonnade
a row of buildings tilted like gravestones
in which a single window is lit
a wall from whose depths shadows emerge
assuming the contours of bodies they will follow
all night and abandon at dawn:
a revelation to you
that each day we take on a new shadow

15.

On the street upturned for an instant
the face of a Siamese princess
a Mayan dancer cross-legged on a bench
Phoenician twins playing flutes beneath a cypress
the populations of lost places still among us
until at nightfall they dissolve in the mist
or assume the forms of animals
to be glimpsed sidelong
a tail a wing a transparent eyelid
just as strangers attempt from passing
impressions to imagine us whole
placing us outside of time:
as immortal as we'll ever get

Robert Desnos in Havana, 1928

The birds with fiery plumage perched
like epaulets on the general's statue
and fountains where girls sun their legs
dipping their toes in the cool ripples
and the shadows of men deep as wells
into which some men fall

A man in a purple suit descends
the gangplank of an ocean liner
carrying a steel suitcase down the boulevard
searching for a single elusive mermaid
and finding them everywhere
lounging in swimming pools by the sea
or dozing atop water towers or rising like Venus
from the claw-foot tub in a tenement

A postman on this zigzag street
is delivering envelopes filled with stars
not of tin foil or paper but the real thing
hissing with radioactivity and glittery
as the diamond dust from Angola
that the lady chauffeurs sprinkle in their hair
when they crash a masquerade ball or visit
the kiosks where aliases are sold like lottery tickets

The neighborhoods in which even the mermaids
disguise themselves as nurses and housewives
their gills pulsing under breezy dresses
or as ushers with scales glinting in gloomy theaters
or lovelorn widows prowling
the fish market with glazed eyes

At the penny arcade a weeping calypso dancer
clouds her spyglass scanning the Caribbean

while orphans pitch coins in the shade
of pink buildings and the whores stand
like sentinels one to a doorway awaiting
sailors with phrase books and off-duty detectives
and even a few of those travelers
just arrived at the aerodrome

who claim to be searching for universal truths
in the hammocks outside fishermen's shacks
and the train station where flower vendors
communicate in the language of bees
and the vacant lots where canine philosophers
of the school of Diogenes are congregating

But who is to say the answers they seek
are not to be found in the landscape that fills
our heads when we face our real moment of truth
for Robert Desnos the twenty-second of February 1944
when the Gestapo knock at his door in Paris
and ship him to Buchenwald where he reads the palms
of his fellow prisoners recites poems and records his
    dreams
of mermaids in notebooks bound for the furnaces

Sixteen years earlier skirting the sea spray
on the promenade could he have foreseen those men
with hammers and pliers for hands
who force us to sign confessions in our own blood
and lead us away with viselike grips
smashing our bones as it pleases them
could he have imagined that for him
it would be this vista of Havana that materialized

A violet sky edged with flames against which a cat
reposes on a Doric column its eyes reflecting
the spinning jigsaw of the city at noon

when the music of the flies in the butcher stalls
hits an impossibly high note demented and never-ending
as the silence in the vault of the National Library
that holds certificates of birth and death
and for initiates only the detailed maps of heaven and hell

Ultima Thule

At the edge of the world
where Ocean begins and ends
the great serpent consuming its own tail

where the purple sun never sets
and oarsmen in galleys cough blood
like sprays of lace freezing on the wind

where starlight fissures the icebergs
and a black cloud that is leviathan himself
hovers on the seafloor

surfacing one night as an island
in the dreams of a Spartan queen
a widow at twenty alone in her bed

who suddenly finds herself wandering this island
vast as a continent which a man walking
every day of his life could not cross

•

When drums awaken her at dawn
the queen watches the revellers-turned-supplicants
paint-smeared and bleary-eyed climb

the steep alleys through a maze of tenements
past sleepless crowds angry children cripples &
    hunchbacks
around the ashes of mountainous bonfires

to the temple where oxen clatter
on the black tiles
and the ax blade touched to a grindstone

throws up a veil of sparks
and the marble basin is scoured
before catching its river of blood

◆

A man cross-legged on a boulder
above a nest of vipers plays a flute
a sinuous melody he heard a woman humming

in the marketplace as she swept by
so that he caught only a glimpse
of her white dress and black hair

and the shock of her red kerchief
that kept flashing before him
when he picked apples from a pyramid

◆

Rendering the queen in limestone
the ghostly gesture with which she beckons
an invisible companion to her side

the sculptor has distilled the essence
of the empire in decline
a ripeness inappropriate to winter

a hollow beneficence
and a bravado better left to another time
another queen

more beloved of the mob
more subtly attuned to the king
her stars so propitious she can do no wrong

◆

On a dirt floor priests indistinct
as their footprints arrange charred bones
and toss pebbles attempting to decipher

the fate of a fleet commander
who disappeared seeking a passage
at the northern mouth of Ocean

where the ice is thick
as two men standing one atop the other
miles of it streaming

off the end of the earth
beneath a sky in which the commander
found no familiar constellations

just a quarter moon a milk-white sun
and a comet that foretold the end
of the world he had left behind

◆

Ghosts perched on rooftops
bridges and parapets
watch the girls dance in the square

silken flowers behind their ears
and sandals of mist on their feet
as they slide back and forth in a long chain

and stare at the clear sky
white clouds sailing across their eyes
blowing out to sea

◆

The queen's innermost chamber
lies at the center of a labyrinth
no man can find

corridors adorned with mirrors and tapestries
the urns of her husband's ancestors
and frescoes depicting the gods at play

Apollo pursuing Daphne through the woods
Zeus and Leto coupling in the form of quails
Poseidon turning himself into a stallion

to ravish Demeter transformed into a mare
a dizzying series of such scenes
culminating in a portrait outside her bedroom

of the queen herself costumed as Artemis
hair wild bow in hand and one slender foot
resting on a stag with an arrow through its heart

♦

In the book that catalogs lost books across time
one entry has been deleted
a volume recently recovered that chronicles

a failed expedition in the great expanse
beyond Ocean from which a lone sailor
returned frostbitten and feverish

to report his fleet blown off course
shipwrecked eventually on the moon
where he claimed a few survivors gazed down

briefly on the gods themselves
an unforgiveable transgression
before freezing to death

◆

An old man who has traveled since dawn
over two rivers and a rocky plain
into the heart of the city

unloads plums pears and apples for the vendors
and a yellow pomegranate
for the deaf girl by the fountain

(drawing pigeons in flight
on a plank
with a bit of charcoal)

then curls up in his two-wheeled cart
beneath a burlap bag
his mule standing asleep in blinding sunlight

◆

At the banquet the queen can observe
friends and enemies commingling
over the bowls of wine and platters of meat

tepidly embracing exchanging pleasantries
harmonious in their disdain
for anyone outside the court

all those citizens consigned
to the coarser precincts of the night
taverns public baths brothels

who will never witness the festivities in this hall
roving clowns and jugglers
the magician who can conjure up a pride of lions

and when the torches are extinguished
to beating drums and clashing cymbals
the lewd acrobats with sweat flying off their backs

who reenact scenes from the private lives
of the gods after which the queen
retires to her quarters with a trio of eunuchs

♦

The royal cartographer sent to Libya
reports manticores roaming
beneath a sky livid with veins and arteries

and the same beating heart for a sun
that drove his predecessor insane
he too charged with drawing

an immutable line across the roughest country
defining for centuries to come
the utmost reach of the queen's authority

a landscape of blood-filled lakes
fiery whirlwinds and the shadows cast
by thousands of propped-up corpses

the warriors who perished
trudging over broken stone
clutching coins imprinted with the visage

of the late lamented king
a snake issuing from his mouth
like the open letter to future generations

he dictated on his death bed
addressing our fears by compounding them
with threats and denials

messengers dispatched to those provinces
all of us come to know in the end
where the roads are paved with bone and lined with
    thorns

◆

Looking in vain for portents the queen
instead discovers the last of her lying generals
emerging from a blue mist

in dented armor and a bloody tunic
a plumed helmet beneath his arm
as he reports the destruction

of all her legions but one
returning home in a lightning storm
encircling the city the palace her private chambers

prepared to defend her
not from the barbarians she so fears
but the people

◆

In the smoke of twilight
the dancer on the whitewashed steps
hugs her knees

the doorway behind her bloodstained
a sparrow picking seeds from wet clay
dogs scuffling on a hill of ashes

a snake charmer opening the basket
from which a python slithers skyward
its eyes pinpoints of green light

while a fire eater finishes his breakfast
of pomegranate juice and pepper tea
flames dancing off his fingertips

his feet smoldering
and the dancer rises slowly
shivering with pain and enters the crowd

learning to maintain her balance again
to skirt the fleet-footed shadows of the dead
to walk without touching the ground

•

The drunken sailor keeping watch
on a promontory
for an overdue ship

scans the horizon until dawn
the clouds that could be islands
and the islands that are clouds

and when nothing appears
he downs another flagon of bitter wine
all week he keeps drinking

a candle stuck on a broken oar
burning at his feet
and a sea bird with the wingspan

of a small island
circling his body watching it
disappear beneath the blown sand

•

The queen looks down
first into one hand
then the other

as if from high in the sky
she is studying a river valley
delicate tributaries crossing her palm

a map that to the trained eye
might reveal her fate
the confluence of forces exerted

by strangers and intimates alike
the remote incendiary incidents
that have changed the course of her life

before and after the king's death
up to and including this moment
when stepping from her perfumed bath

reaching for the gown draped
over the wing of an ivory flamingo
she turns to study herself

in the clouded mirror her hair
dripping onto the cold mosaic
of a phoenix ringed with setting suns

     ✦

When the ghost ship enters the harbor
flying a flag bleached
whiter than snow

its transparent crew files on deck
with heads bowed and tangled hair
to drop their anchor

through fast currents
to the seafloor
where the lost souls cling to driftwood

and nothing lasts for long
not plants or coral
not this anchor forged of ice

     ✦

Drawing into the dusk
the cartographer discovered his lines
took on a life of their own

flowing off the page
looping crisscrossing
and entangling him like a net

a fish in the desert gasping
pleading for mercy
from the merciless gods

     ✦

A scrawny girl attends the general's corpse
bathing and shaving him
oiling his hair rubbing herbs into his skin

she pries open his eyelids
searches his pupils
for the afterglow of that spirit

which once flew
over mountains and seas
to the farthest regions

a man who commanded forty legions
attracting flies through the window
a reminder for those who need it

•

An impartial observer
the scribe attending the ambassador
of a distant court records the spectacle

of war-scarred troops battling
a furious mob
ignorant of the fact the woman

they are protecting is a suicide
sprawled beside her bed
with a knife in her chest

and an asp coiled in her hair
its clear eyelids
revealing human eyes

•

It was left to those Greeks who became one
with the golden dust they kicked up
crossing Persia and Scythia into India

to wander the blank spaces that rimmed their maps
and find even its wonders
chimeras griffons and gorgons unremarkable

who finally reached the point where every unfinished
    journey
(all those dotted lines)
if allowed to continue would converge

a place which for most of us remains elusive
the glowing horizon
that with every step we take recedes another mile

The Woman in the Quarter Moon Kimono

is in fact a man
who has shaved his body
tied back his long hair
and applied whiteface
eyeliner and green lipstick
before parting a curtain
and stepping onstage
to dance around a burning candle

Petals rain down on him
and from behind a screen
(on which a wading stork
dips for carp)
a bamboo flute hits a note
high as the wind that rushes in
off a dark sea
and extinguishes the candle

Slowly he lets down his hair
and removes his kimono
draping it over the screen
so the rays
of its silken moon
reveal a woman's body
slipping into the waves
swimming away from shore

The Desert

The shuttered room is cool
a chair a table a bed on which you stretch out

beneath a mural roughly drawn
of the sky exploding over mountains

one of the landscapes Coyote glimpses
in his journey to the underworld

To arrive here you too traveled many years
abandoned loved ones and learned

secret languages while following
a single road of fire across the plains

Now your shoes are filled with burning sand
your pockets with stones blue as the sky

that were scattered shimmering for miles
when you crossed the mountains

Haiku

Etched on the moth's wings
the story of a man's life
powder to the touch

from ON TOUR WITH RITA (1982)

Double Solitaire

Dark, light, your endless equations
From far out of the past,
From rooms where fine music
Hummed the windowpanes into mirrors
And women with waterfall hair (like yours)
Glided, alone with themselves
But with no one else;
I came to your door with a rain-soaked hat,
My ears ringing with footfalls and bells—
As you pointed out, the streets were silent
And there had been no rain for weeks.

Descartes was your god: the man
Who knew that, if lost, one should leave
The Forest by a straight line only;
From the couch, you graphed me against
A dark wall, all points and lines,
Hands, eyes, and feet a jumble of triangles,
Somehow, eventually, a pattern emerging . . .
After supper, after bed, after the last
Of our long silences, I told you that when Dante
Got lost in your Forest he didn't try to leave.
He knew he was on to something.

Walt Whitman at the Reburial of Poe

". . . of the poets invited only Walt Whitman attended."
—JULIAN SYMONS

They got him in the end, of course.
In a polling booth, dead-drunk.
Vagrant, ballot-stuffer . . .
Four Baltimore coppers to carry that meager frame.
Our first detective of the broken heart,
he picked through its rubble
with his frenzied calculations,
his delirium of over-clarity,
until he found too many clues . . .
Once I dreamt of a man on a schooner,
compact and handsome, alone on the Sound,
thrilling to a violent storm,
threaded to this world by the silver
of a dying spider:
that man was Edgar.
He loved the moon, and the night-torch,
the notion of blood sea-temperatured,
of the cold rush impelling him . . .
In life, in poetry, my antithesis—
detached from the true life,
of rivers and birds and swaying trees,
of soil red with tubers and pregnant clay,
detached from the wondrous release of sex,
his spleen beating heavier than his heart—
two or three men (at least)
packed in among a dozen demons.
He never much cared for my work.
I admired only a fraction of his.
But I happened to be in Washington

last night . . . and I'm old now, half-wise,
too old not to have a sixth sense—
for the genuine article, anyway . . .
I marvel at all he accomplished
in such a hatched life,
electrifying his losses,
celebrating the deer park, the potter's field,
as I celebrated forest and plain . . .
But then to finish here,
another half-forgotten city,
wearing another man's rags—
a scene he might have written:
streets snaking around him,
steaming and sulphurous,
rain dirty as it left the sky—
one last maze before the foothills of hell . . .
And that polling booth . . .
the drinking pals who dumped him there,
frightened perhaps by that dying wolf's voice;
it strikes me now, the eulogies concluded
(I wouldn't give one and I wouldn't say why),
how appropriate he should go that way,
how perversely American in the end—
a man who had consumed himself with exotica,
green as the Republic itself,
poet of our bloodied ankles and ashen bones,
our cankers and lurid dreams:
I wonder who he voted for.
I wonder if he won.

The Track

At the track the horses run
counterclockwise—against time.
In the fields they scatter

around some central idea
which we impose on them.
The thunder breaks differently

on the plateau than on the mountain;
the mice disappear in odd ways,
the owls make contrary moves,

the trees disclose small variations,
but the rain comes in at the same angle
and the wild horses react in the same way—

rearing, white-eyed, under bolts of lightning . . .
Of course all of these horses run
with the clock when they're relaxed.

They connect us to the horizon
with a chain of dust, but too soon
the chain dissolves, the dust settles,

and the wind flies past us, like fire,
into a field which is always empty,
where all the winners go.

Heat

The first man in the last
row is waving his arms
so they blur a cleaning woman
listening to the recital by the door.
Someone is saying that time is
a broken shore, more light than rock
except in bad weather. Heat. The raft
with the dangling legs and the polyglot
girls; the meridian shadows—just off-
white; the leaping fish with hearts
compact and cold as lemons; the groves
of unfalling fruit, drunks in the ditches.
A forger is working in a back room
on a bill honoring the General's birthday:
mauve flowers wreathing a sweating horse.
A girl who tends the well
and has never left either of the two towns
(three miles apart) swears she has seen
two moons in one sky, swears also that she never
dreams and that her mother was a Red Cross nurse
who took to a ship's carpenter and jumped
off a roof on Christmas Day, Rio, ninety degrees and windy.
Crashing chords. Rachmaninoff's shadow. The glassblower
    faints.
Of our dozen strains of blood only two enter
our head and spring into voice—only one intelligible,
melodic, if you want to call it that. Nobody's moving,
everybody's talking. The lone thermometer on the island
runs the Kelvin scale, indecipherable, but hot.
The haze thickens, the flowers remain odorless,
crowds are occupied at their cross-purposes,
their especial preoccupation with the heat

and after that, of course, with sex. A vagrant girl
shimmies clear of her skirt at the well,
the cleaning woman slinks off with a retired carpenter,
no one cares anymore about the forger
or the General; there are even two moons in the sky
and even the dreamers see them. The air whirls
green and black. It is finally so hot that nothing
melts, not the ice, not the music,
because that would be impossible.
And that man in the last row is gone now,
before the applause, his shredded program
on his seat, on fire.

The Road from Pisa to Florence

The road sizzles before us like a fuse,
through orchards and dust,
past children sliding into pools of shadow.
A woman carrying a baby and a bag of mint
tells us Cellini, Raphael, Michelangelo
passed this way—it's gratifying
to travel such a celebrated oven: no wind,
air thick as smoke, clouds bruised into color . . .
In the evening, beside a hedge with our grappa
and lemons, we watch the girls in loose white
dresses, all hips and sidelong glances,
smiles running like water;
suddenly a dog cuts into a field, the quails rise,
echoes falter, darkness melts the hills.
My friend, a painter, blacks over his lines
and pockets his pad:
"We never see a place," he says,
"Until we leave it behind." Yes,
and by then it has become someplace else.

On the Meridian

Your feints are choreographed . . .
by the ice.
Cactus crowds the red ravine,
lightning bridges the mountains,
yesterday's sky slides in,
solidifying the props—like definitions:
white table with a pestle,
twin plates of shriveled fruit,
salt rimming a glass.
Sitting back, carnation moon
in your lapel, irises changing
color to a metronome click,
you claim that fog carries
the brighter light, rising
behind you and following the slow
bend that rustles like a river
where there is no river.
The other light is still darkening—
the real moon, a half-moon,
making us see half of what we might be.

Rimbaud Crossing the Alps

He's always thought of as a very young man—
Rightly so. In the mountains, past Gstaad,
He sat in a cherry tree and watched the falcons
Hover after the avalanche, dip, glide,
And return to their masters: men on horseback
In the fast mist. He stayed with the widow
In the house by the waterfall, read her
The single slim edition of his poems,
Verlaine's copy, sent from Belgium,
And this when he was on his way to the East,
When he had given up poetry for a bag
Of maps and compasses, for that deluxe
Money belt from Bern: he was ready for gold.
The widow's thighs went from white to red to snow-blue,
Her pale mirror-image made him wince sitting up in bed,
He mouthed some words when her back was turned,
Saw himself clearly for once: a man just beyond
The glaze of the desert, answering to many names,
Spraying the silence with voices, a sky dense
With suns gangrening his legs, gold raining
Onto his chest, the gold of alchemists
Which he feared in his dreams . . .
The widow stoked another fire, loosened her blouse.
She liked to hear this boy talk, hands
Never still, as she combed out his hair,
She liked his shortened breath and his restfulness
When he fell from her and curled up in the morning light . . .
A few days later, some miles higher,
A man on horseback, mist-featured

And wearing white gloves, found him in the snow,
In the blue shadows, out cold, feverish,
And arranged for him to be sent back to France. To die.
The boy was twenty years old.
He would sail east and live another seventeen years.

Nocturne for Miranda

Sky's heavened tonight—
Not for the master, his dome,
His perfect notes off harp-shaped clouds;
Not for any of that,
But for us.
We breathe softly, crosswise,
A half-murmur, a hundred bypassed
Sentences, and still things seem clearer
Most of the time.
There are angels everywhere,
Several of them doing imitations
Of us into the twilight,
All of them bright and formally dressed,
Walking the divisions between stars,
Reclining on meteor tails,
High rollers with the wrists quicker
Than light . . .
Now you see them as well;
In some paintings, you say, they glow
Like shadows in a storm:
Ecstatic, grim, never faltering
But always waiting for the fall.

from *On Tour with Rita*

Busted, throat sandpapered by the wind,
Rita spry as a winter bird rations
The tequila, a shot an hour, ladies first.
She's dreamt there's no water for miles.
Mountains on all sides hazed violet,
Her hair burned gold as the cloud
The hawks halo, a mile up,
Desperate for all their lazy turns,
Scanning the rocks for lizard—
A halo of slashes in a red sky . . .
Rita's restless inside a circle of her footprints,
Squint-eyed and brown, disappointed
That everything surprises her until it happens.

#7 Vermont

Breezes bitter in these hills,
Sunlight avalanching fields
Of corn, insects persisting . . .
Rita there doesn't dislike anything
Except the bats (the white ones) at dusk.
She sits back in dark glasses
Sipping soda water, the dogs
Whining, flattened by the heat.
Come this way with the best intentions,
Virgin notebooks and a bed built
For marathons—she nods off
While ravens with scissor wings
Cut the sky into furling blue sheets.

#II New Year's Day

From the rattle to rattling
Bones—that's neat says Rita
Lying in the snow, hair scattered,
Desert-blonde, out-of-place.
We ride downhill on waxed runners
And never never run out of time
Or snow or night—just breath.
Lungs sop wind, nostrils flare—
But that's not enough.
Even a lover's whistle falls short
When it comes to last gasps.
After the blizzard a man waits
At the foot of the hill
Feeding the bonfire busted sleds.

#13 Boston

Wonderful that she's surviving
The July evenings, suede hat
Pulled to her eyes, the humidity
So dense it could be raining
And no one would know; her cat,
The one that walks in sentences,
Paws at a mirror in the kitchen
While Rita sprawls out, naked cool legs
On the coffee table, a scratchy Ravel
On the phonograph and vodka spilled
Down her breast; her one open eye
Sees string from wrist-to-ceiling, ankle-to-ceiling,
Then she feels her neck for rope, but nothing yet.

From A SHORT HISTORY OF
THE ISLAND OF BUTTERFLIES (1986)

The Public Gardens

Someone might mistake the shadows
of the loners for sleeping animals,
the darting light for a bird of prey.

The palms shiver reflections
across the fountain, and the goldfish
glide through channels of algae.

On wet evenings they jump for
cigarettes or gum; in a drought
they surface belly-up, full of death.

Ancient architects centered this city
around the Public Gardens—the dark
hub to a wheel of radiating streets.

They run fast and straight for miles,
but at the city limits
they go black, they empty.

Around the fountain the weeping willows,
filled with nightingales, glint
like cages in the moonlight.

Under the cones of lampposts,
the statues of nymphs and satyrs
survey the blue trees

where the solitary lovers
and the lost children—
all those who have paid dearly

for their corner of the night—
curl into the shadows
like cats and count the stars.

A single guard is asleep at the gate,
dreaming of the treetops like wavelets
rippling under alpine winds,

and of the city's dead
in garish dress, waving to the statues
from their funeral trains,

and of the river beyond the suburbs
where the boulevards end,
where the air is black and rainy

and the foliage opens like a curtain
onto millions of bright flowers.

Cardiac Arrest

This is the time when the gods come
for your heart.
Down the long blue corridors,
past one door, then another,
a last dark turn and then—
light. Simplicity of motion,
of gestures, in a gallery
of white shadows.
And you dream without sleeping:
of miners who scrape coal
from the earth like roe from a fish;
of the monks in hell
with the lead-lined cloaks;
of obsidian eels at a hundred fathoms
who have witnessed the birth of whales;
of the hands against a golden light
that bathed and combed you
and turned you in your sleep.
You are flat on the sidewalk
of a busy city street
and a crowd has gathered to watch
the policeman loosen your collar.
High, high in the sunlight
a construction crane raises a man
in a cage—a deus ex machina
swaying against the clouds.
Truly, the man could be a god,
rising even higher now, escaping
with your heartbeat in the palm of his hand.

Radium

The black lacquered urn etched with mountains
and glowing stars might best have displayed
camellias on a bedside table.
It holds the ashes of a T'ang prince
killed in an avalanche in his twenty-first year.
Excavated in a uranium mine, two thousand miles
from Peking, estranged from all imperial
relics of that or any other dynasty,
it was buried long enough for the pitchblende's
radium to fleck its luminosity
onto those stars alone.
Now the entire urn is radioactive,
with an astronomical half-life that prevents
meddling by human hands;
so we cannot be sure the prince's
ashes do not also glow—
that small measure of diamond dust
which one winter, as flesh and blood,
crossed the Empire, and on a mountain
crag at the frontier,
upon hearing a rumble above,
murmured his amazement to a silent retainer,
his words glinting for an instant
in the rush of snow.

Construction Site, Windy Night

Great plastic sheets are flapping
twenty stories up, east and south,
where tinted windows will look out
over the park next summer,

and widows will draw their blinds,
and men gripping iced drinks talk
about money and death
while the moon slides between clouds;

and up another ten stories,
the foreman's corrugated shack
rattles, and the rats tip
a pail of rivets onto the floor

where cats will doze, and young
girls waltz, and lovers groan,
oblivious of wild parties above
and children howling below;

and even higher, on the roof,
a flock of pigeons lines the railing,
and they will remain as they are,
scanning the blotted trees

and mating and sleeping
and squinting at the odd visitor
who will venture up on a summer night
to be alone or to meet someone,

to escape an argument
or to connect with the cosmos,
to stare down from that windy perch
at his fellow citizens

crossing streets and hailing cabs
and think how far away they are,
and how the things men construct
in their minds can materialize

suddenly, towering over them
and filling them with dread of heights.

Evening

An old man crosses the wet lawn
at dusk as the swallows dip
between the rows of elms.
He passes through the gate in the hedge,
his boots crowfooted with cut grass,
and his white coat catches the gleam
from an upstairs lamp
as he stops to light a cigar,
which then, like a June bug
on fire, precedes him
through the thistles and brush,
over the salt grass like mermaids' hair
and the tiny highways of the fast crabs,
down to the ragged field by the sea.

The dolphins zigzag, and the seafloor
mirrors up its silver darkness,
and the roses bloom in the clouds
escaping the continent—
but what is it that rivets him
and stirs him to laughter
on that bluff where the breakers'
music, like shrouds of gravel covering
and uncovering the dead, reduces younger
men to taut humility or silence?
An hour passes, and the gulls,
custodians of that slow borderline,
follow him back as far as the gate,
and by then the swallows are perched
and the black owls alert
and the big house ablaze with lights

as the ember of his cigar floats across
the dark lawn, and with a startling cry,
amplified by the quick wind,
the children hiding behind the cold elms
rush out to greet him.

Losing Altitude

Plummeting past the birds,
millions of them flapping by,
the orange cloud bank a warren of ghosts,
of ghostly chatter still audible
above the whine of our twin engines,
our racing four-chambered hearts.

Is this the way to Xanadu—
slicing through the earth in seconds
to emerge upside down in China?
Or, rather, the route Elijah took,
fooling us with mirrors
as he fell to heaven?

There is no way of knowing anything.
And no one here to soothe us.
The only consolation is Zeno's:
each of our few remaining seconds
halved infinitely until we are left
with sunlight, sky, and eternity.

The altimeter keeps the time,
running down to zero o'clock
when the merciful angels
will ring their golden bells
and the flamethrower angels
douse us with immortality.

In these last miles the air
thickens to blue mist
riddled with flickering windows
in which impassive faces ebb and flow,
peering past their own shadows,
all of them vaguely familiar . . .

A lifetime of faces, from cities
we walked, stations and terminals,
all the journeys that led us here—
without parachutes or prayers—
where the white sea rushes up
at breakneck speed to welcome us.

Lineage

Here's a photograph taken in Manhattan in 1891.
From a rooftop looking south
on the first day of summer.
A man with a cane is smoking in a doorway,
watching a woman alight from a carriage.
A dog is crouching at his heels.
The flags are at half-mast.
In the distance, in Union Square, construction is underway
on another office building,
and some falling bricks just scattered the pigeons.
It was the year before my grandfather was born.
The clock on the bank reads 9:30.
Across from the bank is a theater.
On the sidewalk a vendor is examining a peach
and a policeman is gazing at the sky.
Two boys are rolling a hoop under the marquee.
All of them are dead now.

That same day my great-grandmother was on her honeymoon.
Sitting by the window of the bridal suite
in a hotel ringed with fiery bougainvillea
Her husband is asleep on the couch
under a thick shadow.
She has wrapped his jacket around her shoulders.
She is seventeen years old.
Eight months later she will die in childbirth,
but her son—my grandfather—will survive.
Eventually, he will settle in Manhattan.
My father and I will be born there,
and I will write this poem there on a summer day,
on another rooftop.

In the photograph there is also a girl in a hotel window.
She is looking directly at the photographer, through the
    sunlight.
She is pale, her eyes are wide,
and she resembles my future wife.
The clock on the bank still reads 9:30,
but it appears some in the crowd have moved:
the vendor has pocketed the peach
and the man with the dog is crossing the street
and the boys' hoop is lying in the gutter.
The girl in the window has changed, too.
Her face has darkened and her gaze is averted—
as if someone has called to her from across the room.
Across the years.

The House Where Lord Rochester Died

The embarrassment of the swans
in the bedroom mural fleeing
the milkmaids in the satyr's bath;

and the storm clouds—rendered
so delicately by well-paid hands—
creeping westward, trailing the orgy;

and the orchids still moist
and flush in the cherub's mouth . . .
In this mural, as out the bay window,

the prospect of rain appears endless,
the hayfield swirls with pollen—
the vistas merge across time.

This confusion of nature and art,
overlapping so casually,
leaves us dizzy as we back out of the room,

through the padded doors and down
the icy stairwell, across a gallery
of spidery light where we find,

fired in dust on a bare wall,
the imprint of a man
shielding his eyes, wiping his mouth.

Leaving Town

The trumpeter in the mariachi band
dreamt again of a landlocked swan.

Of the blue desert
under a moon filled with seawater.

The drummer overslept as usual
and the band left him behind.

They were staying in the hotel
with the broken fountain.

Last night the drummer posed for pictures
with the girls at the Triangle Club.

This was between the band's two sets
at the Café Barracuda, next door.

The trumpeter also missed the train
this morning, but for personal reasons.

He had glimpsed a woman he used to know
(her hair dyed black) getting off an elevator.

The two musicians ate lunch
downtown, at a chop-suey joint.

In the distance the mountains
shimmered behind the desert wind.

The drummer recounted his evening's adventures,
but the trumpeter wasn't listening.

He was thinking back on old times
with the woman—another city, another life.

A July afternoon of flatbed trucks
rushing by with slabs of ice.

And crazy sirens. And a dozen people
dead of heat exhaustion. And endless quarrels.

All the same quarrel, about a woman
who had lied to both of them and run away.

That night they had gone to the park
and watched the river through the elms.

Separately, they counted the sapphires
the moonlight was laying on the far bank.

The drummer, weary of talking, bought some cigars
and asked the waiter where he could score opium.

Then he wired ahead to the band in the next town
and reserved two seats on the train.

The trumpeter called the hotel
and left a message for the woman.

Later, at the station, he told
the drummer he was quitting the band.

The drummer wished him luck
and borrowed ten dollars.

The trumpeter bought a bouquet of roses
and returned to the hotel.

At the desk they told him the woman had received
his message, and left town on the afternoon train.

The Partisan

I was eating black olives in the sun
when the bullets whistled through my heart
and I heard children singing.
I glimpsed soldiers behind the rocks,
but my last impression was of my wife,
whose hair was blonde as the field
flying away from under me.
Even as a student I had prepared myself
for that day, the hour I would be led
to a stained wall or makeshift gallows,
blindfolded with set jaw and clenched fists;
I never imagined I might be ambushed
over my lunch, years after my last skirmish,
temples graying and old wounds blued into scars;
I had not even a delusion of my own martyrdom.
No followers, no weapon in my belt:
how they found me, why they were still pursuing,
and what price lay on my head, I'll never know.
I hadn't read a newspaper in years.
Nor spoken to a single soul.
I remembered the streets of the capital,
not as a maze of police and barricades,
but with nostalgia, with a boy's memory
of carnivals and parades, of my father
at the edge of a crowd smoking his white pipe.
In hiding, I devoured books on medicine and astronomy,
Pliny and Galen, Kepler and Galilei.
For a while, I considered going abroad.
Too late.
They buried me on the spot, in my boots and hat,
carpeting the grave with pine needles and stones,
blending them carefully into the texture of the hillside.

As if nothing had happened.
Rifling my pockets, closing my eyes,
they overlooked but one detail:
my mouth which never opened again,
which clamped shut with an olive pit under the tongue;
even now, I am waiting for the tree that will one day
burst forth, casting its shadow in my image—
plunging them into darkness.

Reflections on a Bowl of Kumquats, 1936

The exemplar of the calculating squint
and the surreptitious kick to the shin,
of the fight to the finish, no holds barred;
the juggler with billiard balls and oranges,
interchangeable in a blur—
like Life&Death at the heart of the farce:
bite into the wrong thing in the dark and watch
the teeth fly like sparks, everybody laughing . . .
Sly, slyer than cats and lady druggists,
more familiar than house dicks with the bright evil
gritted into the fabric of things, of "everyday life,"
so many places to avoid, and dreams,
the man in the four-way mirror outflanking his insomnia,
pockets stuffed with bankbooks,
closely shaven even at 2 A.M.
Let double-talk patch the fearsome wind,
a crazy quilt of insults and anxious asides,
only the children, who threatened him, equipped
to read the barometer of that face,
the short degrees between spite and rage,
degrees of applause and betrayal,
of the dinginess of rooms, of the lost years
notched with a penknife on his traveling trunk.
Now see the sun setting behind the palms,
see the weedless lawn and the Florentine fountain,
see the clay court steaming through the vines,
see Hollywood to the north dirty and pink;
tailored in white with rakish Panama, chewed corona,
the nimble fat man sips gin from a halved tennis ball,
shows the vicious backhand patented for laughs, for winning.
Only the stray dogs at the gate can appreciate that.
Never give a sucker an even break.

Winter Night

Burning torches line the floor of the sea.
Women in white hurry along the beach,
into the mist, with a pack of dogs.
It is past midnight.
Airplanes, every few minutes, fly out from the land,
over the bluffs where the stripped trees
line up like crosses in a military graveyard.
A lighthouse beams its small yellow moon onto the breakers,
and the big moon hangs behind scudding clouds.
The women pause at the jetty and loosen their hair.
The dogs leap through the surf with muffled cries
and run in circles around the dim figures
that have appeared in the shallows:
men with smoky faces and limbs,
robed in sheets of blue light.
The women stare past them, mesmerized by the torches.
The airplanes are growing louder, and more frequent.
It is cold and the gray sand has slicked itself into glass.
The women skate back up the beach against the whistling wind,
and the dogs dive through the black curtain where the water
    deepens,
and the men disappear in a burst of spray.
The torches float up to the surface, like the reflections of stars.
On the bluffs, the trees still resemble crosses in a graveyard.
It is a graveyard.
Across the sea the war has ended.
Those were the airplanes gone to fetch the wounded.
Those were the dead, watching the waves come in.

The Milky Way from Brenda's Lawn

The Lone Ranger used to his ride his horse
Silver down that glittering road.
Pythagoras mapped it out for him.
Outlaws, behind boulders, fired black
bullets into the night, hoping for
their small share of notoriety,
and made the mistake of their lives.
A thirst for evil (with its adrenal kick)
lured them to shallow graves
on a distant moon—silver bullets,
like stars, lodged in their hearts.

Brenda is singing to the silver owls
in the apple orchard, waiting for
them to swoop up across the sky.
She's been watching the luxury liners
sail in from deep space along
their gulfstream of crushed diamonds.
I tell her that the Milky Way is too many
stars to count, more than all the people
who have ever lived or died,
and that none of us can expect more
than a single star to shine truly
in our eyes, our hearts, on the tip
of our tongues, before we're gone.

Jeoffry the Cat

The pale fields flow like the sea
in the darkening light.
Jeoffry keeps watch over me,
the two of us balanced
on the scales of the living God.
I drop to my knees
as the deadly moon alights
on the black hill
and the soft armies gather.
I see them there seeing me.
A man in London with a telescope
has cataloged my every sin.
Smart, Christopher. *Insanus.*
My heart is one star
he will never chart,
its lick of white flame blackening.
Jeoffry has seen the birds
of paradise in far galaxies,
the revolutions of dying suns,
the flickering angels in orchestra;
seen it all, unamazed,
in the fix of his jeweled eye.
I must not feed him meat or fowl.
Nor scraps of human prayer.
Nor slop of human desire.
Within these walls beating,
our two hearts merge
their singing chambers.
Our keeper, long fallen
to his present state, gapes
at me and asks what I scribble
each dawn staring southward.

A song of that red meadow,
I whisper, where the blind girls
dance their ancient step.
A song no one will hear.
Only Jeoffry hears the bells
that ring dark and light
in the fast skies of creation.
Jeoffry who licked the Baptist's head
and curled round Jesus' foot
by the lepers' well.
I am a mad Englishman,
more hound than jaguar,
more highwayman than cleric,
more brokenhearted than they suspect.
I eats the leavings.
I writes the pauses.
I bathes with hard wine.
Jeoffry he crosses this cell
fused with holy intelligence
and airy health,
his forepaws lifted
to the burning air.
When I die they must let him
to the road, his mission,
to grace the original rhythm
of the ringing of dark and light,
the glass road that spirals
and may not end,
that I shall never see.

Musical Chairs

You start with the dancing girls,
move on from there.

Bouquets, incense, endless games
of musical chairs in the clouds.

After some years, your tread loses
its spring, your hand its sweep,

the words that leapt in persuasion
barely float on the narrowing stream.

It is at this point the great diarists err:
turning to religion, or drugs.

Turning, with brackish concurrence,
to a jaded sea, the salt and sleet

that whirls out memories.
And the vapors of regret,

and sorrow in the charting of tides,
and the open wound marbled and elegized—

like all deep-sea monuments,
designed to misguide the young,

to sustain the supremacy
of that old port of call.

Where the gamesters play for hearts
with a shaved deck.

Where the music accelerates
and the chairs disappear.

You start with the dancing girls.
They never let you go.

From DESPERATE CHARACTERS (1988)

Krazy Kat

Playing the bongos in Rome,
dancing the rumba in Reykjavik—
he's seen it all, from Oslo to Oman.

From the tarot deck, he always draws
the Knave of Batons:
trustworthy and doomed to misadventure.

He's so wired, with so many outlets
into the expanding universe,
that he can't connect with anyone anymore.

On a supersonic jet over the Sahara,
Mahler rumbling on his earphones,
he sets up his magnetic chess set.

From memory, he plays out Alekhine's
famous victory over Capablanca at Leiden
in 1938, using the French Defense.

He can still smell dates frying in oil
at the bazaar in Rabat, and he can taste
the wind flooding the medina, dark as honey.

But he hasn't talked to a soul in days.
His pockets are filled with cigarettes,
candy bars, and maps of the seafloor.

Once he owned a globe of Mars—
its mountain ranges cleverly embossed—
charted as minutely as the USA.

So when the first astronaut zips across
the red planet in his dune buggy
he'll know exactly where he's going.

Everything will have a name.
Like this lissome stewardess behind her veil.
And the desert below. And the pink stars.

At the airport in Tunis he drinks
mint juleps in the empty VIP lounge;
twice in two weeks the place has been bombed.

Cops in mufti eye him closely
in his black Stetson, puffing a corona,
a copy of the Koran in his hip pocket.

He's just skimmed the first chapter—
"Thick Blood, or Clots of Blood"—
trying to find the epigrams the terrorists use.

Four thousand years ago Pharaoh's cats gazed on
the blue world and cried for grief all night.
Krazy Kat can relate to this.

In the name of Allah, the compassionate, the merciful:
in the end how do we know one desert from another,
and how do we remember our own names?

He's sure that on Mars those red canals
flow south to north, like the Nile,
thick as lava and cold as human blood.

Green Animals

You can glimpse them at twilight
in the vague terrain surrounding
the ancient stadium after it rains;
or on the cupola's copper dome,
weathered the acid-green of the sea
at dawn, before the storm comes.

When they stare back at you,
you see the eyes of your ancestors glittering,
their familiar forms unlike those
you imagined for the dead
in their sky-locked rooms;
you see yourself in those blurred settings,
before a forest backdropped with mountains.
Beyond all that, and beyond still
more mountains and an emerald sea,
lies a greener landscape
from which the animals have fled
in a vast cloud, like ghosts.
Call it death, something permanent,
as you listen to the rain approaching
fast across the hollow rooftops.

Collecting Stamps in Port-au-Prince

Here's another dictator with a bright blue
parrot on his shoulder, white top hat, and sash
blazing forth the colors of the Republic.
A departure from those tedious series of sailboats,
sunsets, and gay fishermen that enchanted the previous rulers.
This fellow's grandfather, onetime "emperor," with a retinue
of forty pugilists in baseball caps and sunglasses,
was a good friend to the orphans of the capital
and every Christmas presented them with shoes and socks,
then picked out the prettiest girl, took her
to the honeymoon suite of the King James Hotel,
and kept her in thrall for a year.
He had forty-seven such brides during his reign
which ended when No. 4, an aging consumptive,
emerged from obscurity and shot him in the confession box.
His son and grandson were never so careless.
They didn't advertise their peccadilloes,
rarely attended church, and never confessed to anything.
When they issued commemorative sheets to trumpet
the virtues of their regimes, they kept them simple:
banana trees in pink sunlight, canoeists in dusky lagoons,
jai alai players, and flattering self-portraits.
The son was himself an amateur collector;
he hosted the first Transcaribbean Philatelic Convention,
and his albums are displayed at the National Museum
alongside his sabers, crowns, and the 689 medals
for valor he awarded himself.
Every year on her birthday he decreed a stamp
to honor his wife, a former cabaret hostess,
costumed variously as Pallas Athena and Marie Antoinette.
The grandson (the one with the parrot) in the end
went kinky, like his grandfather, manning a destroyer

with an all-girl crew, bathing beauties in seamen's uniforms,
and chasing them around the deck by moonlight;
he drowned on one such outing, wrestling two "mermaids,"
and, miraculously, when his body washed up the next morning,
it was festooned with orchids and surrounded by dolphins,
his white admiral's uniform still crisp and dry.
Even today his sinister countenance,
under that top hat, sees every letter on the island,
from the rustiest post box on the remotest country lane,
to its ultimate destination, worldwide,
though most of the stamps are so gorgeously intricate
that the addressee forgets to open his mail,
oddly reminding us of those old movies
in which the dizzy blonde or the mischievous upstart
sticks a rare stamp on an envelope
and hands it to the mailman so the comedy might begin,
the complex machinations of recovering the stamp
before it is postmarked, while the letter within
(which might contain crucial information—
of lost love or riches or intrigue)
is utterly forgotten.

Elegy for My Grandmother

Now you're in the place where the shadows fly,
light-years away from this palm forest—
the room I've taken overlooking the Caribbean,
macaws squawking at the stars
and coconuts thudding to earth.

At your old house the garden lies barren;
lightning split the cherry tree,
black vines choked the azaleas.
You were famous for your green thumb.
Neighbors brought you their ailing plants,
and after a week on your terrace
the puniest amaryllis turned prodigy.
Your bags were always packed:
you loved to travel first class, to sail
south at the first sign of winter.
I have a photograph of you in prewar Havana
wearing a white coat and feathered hat
after a day at the races,
gazing to sea (these same flashing waters)
from the casino balcony.
I remember you were cursed
with eyesight so sharp it daggered
migraines through your temples.
Once, driving in the country, you glanced
at a distant line of trees on a mountain slope
and counted the crows on a single bough.

You were first onto the dance floor
when the music started—and last to sit.
Before I could read, you taught me
poems and riddles, and those intricate
parables with the quirky endings—

your own variations on some theme.
You knew the real theme is always death,
and when I was ten you explained it to me:
one is on an enormous ship
(lush gardens lining the decks)
gliding over a white sea that never ends.
There is no horizon, no sun or moon:
the air is purest light.
The portholes are mirrors,
full of glittering expanses.
Somewhere on board an orchestra
is playing beautiful music,
but no one can find the musicians . . .

Now that you're a passenger on that ship,
sailing and sailing into the light,
are they playing for you
on a dance floor strewn with flowers,
and is the music really so beautiful?
Nana, this was your way of telling me
you would never come back.

Christmas, 1956

They had him on a velveteen throne
in the toy department
beside a metal tree
sprayed with aerosol snow.
His cheeks were rouged
and there was a whiff
of onion on his breath
and a cookie crumb
stuck in his beard.
He looked like a man
who enjoyed boilermakers
and hero sandwiches
with all the trimmings.
He was nearsighted,
deep crow's-feet forking
from his washed-out eyes.
When he rang his bell,
we filed in one at a time,
sat on his lap,
and were photographed
by a skinny woman
dressed as an elf
who talked to herself.
I liked that he wore white
gloves with tiny buttons;
I liked his shiny belt
with the silver buckle.
But his boots were all wrong.
They weren't boots at all:
around his calves, above
scuffed, rubber-sole shoes,
he had fastened black

plastic cylinders with zippers.
He sported a watch, too,
with a radium dial
and a chromium Speidel band
that pinched his pudgy wrist.
A star-traveler such as he
(our first astronaut?),
able to navigate unerringly
in dead of night,
should have had no need
of such a primitive timepiece.
I told him what I wanted
him to bring me—
listed according to preference—
and he listened absently,
squinting into the light,
then gave me a candy cane
and sent me on my way.

Riding home, I figured that
even though every big store
in every city in America
employed one of these imposters,
though there must be thousands
of them with pillows
strapped around their waists
and fake beards glued
to their chins,
one and only one
(free to operate in secrecy
because of all his decoys)
had to be real.

Map

My great-grandfather was beached
in the tropics on Christmas Day, 1870,
redirecting the family destiny
(the geography shifted, the genes darkened);
still adrift at the end of a long life,
surrounded by mute children, he died
in a bamboo room, behind mosquito netting,
listening to his wife's chimes.
I visit his grandfather's hometown,
walk the narrow streets he walked,
loiter in the church where he was baptized,
married, and buried, where the icy statues
of the angels that survey the pews
were modeled on his twin daughters,
lost in a blizzard only to resurface
in Africa, as missionaries;
I have their picture tucked into my notebook,
blonde girls in severe coats, smiling.
Exploring the town, I feel as if I have
touched down from another planet;
it's hard to connect with these ghosts
whose blood fills my veins.
I cannot imagine what they would make of me,
unshaven, speaking a strange language,
dust-caked on a motorcycle.
The red sun burns slowly.
Snow shrouds the hills in lace.
Tucked into the river bottom,
fish sleep the winter wound
in filaments of ice, like mummies.
On my last night, I examine a crude map,
crayoned in blue, passed down to me

from a man dead two centuries,
whose name I carry, and whom
I am said to resemble:
it describes the coordinates of a lake,
a barren field, and the stone house
an even remoter ancestor abandoned
to come to this town.
If I were to search it out
(and circle the lake, cross the field),
where would that take me
and what shadows would I stir
and who would be there telling me
I could never escape the past?
Telling me I could never leave.

From IN THE YEAR OF THE COMET (1992)

Outside Perpignan in Heavy Rain

The trees sway darkly
along the black wall with its vines.
For shelter, a cat squeezes
between the steel bars over a window.
This is where the caretaker lives,
catty-corner to the cemetery,
with a door the color of stone.

We've just descended the mountains,
windshield wipers slapping mud
while we talked about the acrobat
who was in the papers in Barcelona
yesterday: how he attempted
to perch blindfolded on the highest
steeple of the Gaudí cathedral.

Through the gate, in the first
row of gravestones, a statue
depicts a young woman
raising her hand to her face:
the mortuary sign for a suicide.
Is she about to touch her forehead?
to tear out her hair?
to dig her nails into her cheek?
to stifle a cry
or make the sign of the cross?

In this life which is the only life
it is a gesture we see every day.
You say someone in a position
to know told you it's easy
to learn about these things

without learning anything at all.
Without ever running out of questions.
When that acrobat fell in bright sunlight,
did all the women in the street raise
their hands to shield their eyes?

Green Chair on a Fire Escape in Autumn

In summer a girl sat
there every afternoon
in a yellow bikini,
fedora, and wraparound
sunglasses, oblivious of
the traffic, skimming
magazines, smoking Cheroots
and sipping Campari
beside her calico cat
who dozed on the windowsill
beneath the cloud-print
curtains while pale clouds
sailed out to sea
and the sun blasted
the bricks so hard dawn
to dusk that a fine red
dust swirled the streets.

Until one day she moved
away, taking the curtains
and the cat but leaving
her chair—still facing
southward to catch
the rays of the sun
which no longer rose high
enough to clear the water
towers of the building
across the street;
and this morning when
a sudden downpour
stopped me under an awning,
and the chair, spattered

with yellow leaves, shone
like fresh enamel against
the dull sky, I wished
she were sitting there
again, startled by the rain
into glancing down
for once, just long enough
to reveal her eyes,
which must be green.

Reading the Sunday Comics, Summer 1963

1. Gasoline Alley

Smiling young men with bulging biceps
who change your flat tire
and never dirty their white coveralls.
The girl from the coffee wagon
in her checkered apron
who leans against the soda machine
happily chewing gum.
No one having sex.
Or wanting it.
Lawns and flowerbeds without weeds
set back on tree-lined streets.
Everything orderly.
Every surface polished.
Every human being as easy
to take apart and reassemble
as a car engine.
A universe of cleanly moving parts
that would have pleased Descartes.
So that, after lunch, at the baseball field,
a boy washing down chocolate bars
with chocolate milk
will rub his rabbit's foot
and pitch a no-hitter
into the ninth inning
of a scoreless game
and then lose it on a bloop single.
Good-naturedly learning a moral lesson.
Then going home to find
a hot supper waiting for him.
On both sides of the railroad tracks

a community of honest men
doing an honest day's work.
No one dying.
Someone always telling a familiar joke
in the end, while the sun sets,
and everybody laughing.

2. Blondie

The harried, hysterical housewife
in need of a therapist
in a world where there is no therapy.
Her husband the diligent oaf,
with hair parted down the middle,
who is afraid of his boss.
Her daffy daughter and bumbling son,
who could be youthful twins
of their parents.
She forgets things everywhere:
hats and handbags,
pancakes on the skillet,
irons burning holes in shirts.
She likes bubble baths on hot afternoons.
She shops.
Late at night, when she's taken off
her polka-dot dress
and put on a polka-dot robe,
her husband is making one of his famous
sandwiches, sixteen inches high
(salami, baloney, cheese and onions,
olives, eggs, bacon and pickles),
in the brightly lit kitchen
with the half-moon nestled in the window.

She pours herself a glass of milk
and sits at the table
to watch him eat.
Nothing will ever change for her.
Just once, she would like to sleep
in the nude—with someone else.

3. Betty and Veronica

Two girls driving by a sparkling lake
in a red convertible.
Listening to rock and roll.
Combing their hair.
Eating cheeseburgers and drinking shakes
without ever losing their figures.
One a blonde, the other a brunette.
Carefree and flirtatious.
With beautiful teeth.
They will never witness a crime
or enter a voting booth.
Never go to college
or work in an office
or feel their youth slip away.
Never suffer the griefs
of childbirth, illness or divorce.
For all eternity
boys in letter sweaters
will give them signet rings
and fight for the privilege
of taking them
to drive-ins and proms.
In a life of perpetual sunshine
they never sleep, never tire,

their eyes wide with an astonishment
that never ends.
A kind of passion.

4. Dondi

The brooding orphan boy
passed among strangers
who live in gloomy houses.
His suitcase always packed.
His wide mournful eyes.
His blue-black hair with the cowlick.
His life that is a progression
of darkening adjectives.
His dog who is also ineffably sad.
Where will Dondi end up
and how alone will he be,
forever choking back tears
cold as water cupped from deep
in the North Atlantic.
It pained me
that I never liked him.

Epitaph on a Dictator

He was wearing a white tie,
cream-colored suit,
and no blindfold
when they led him
before a firing squad
on Christmas Day
in a rubbled courtyard
full of starving chickens.
All his ministers were forced
to drink strychnine
while handcuffed together
in a meat freezer.
For twenty-four years
he kept a clove of garlic
over his heart, on a chain,
to ward off the Evil Eye,
and he had the National
Orchestra play Wagner
when he swam laps
in the floating natatorium
on his private lake.
His office with its fifty-foot
ceiling and marble pillars
was adorned with six portraits,
twelve busts, and a mural
of himself (heroic on a
battlefield), and his dozens
of uniforms, rainbowed with
medals, hung wrinkle-free
in a refrigerated closet.
In the "out" box on
his desk there were

closeups of naked girls.
(Had the "in" box at some
point contained photos
of the same girls clothed?)
He was a gun collector
and voyeur extraordinaire
(entire brothels monitored
by his secret cameras)
and also a connoisseur of jade,
with predictably expensive
tastes in Scotch, sports
cars, and all things silk.
He boasted he would never
have changed places
with any man anywhere,
even born as he was
in a dirt-floor shack
on the lip of a swamp
with bluebottle flies
dancing around his head.
At the stroke of noon,
under a gunmetal sky,
while the statues of him
in every town and city
were being dynamited,
he died unrepentant
for the thousands
executed in his prisons
and torture chambers,
for the billions of francs
in Swiss banks he had
bled from his citizens,
for the children in work camps
(the lucky ones)

and the others stricken
with polio and AIDS,
died wetting his pants
with three words on his lips:
"Trust no one."

Mrs. Luna

Think of an address you've known
for many years, embedded
in your memory—mantra-like—
belonging to a distant
aunt or uncle
whom you've never visited
but to whom you send
a card at Christmas
and from whom you receive
neatly wrapped packages
on your birthday;
or the address of a former
lover or long-lost
friend residing on
an exotically named street
(Royal Alhambra Boulevard)
in an unlikely town
(Nocturne, South Dakota).
It is just such an address
(for you, the abstraction
of a place)
that one day you find
yourself standing before:
a stucco bungalow
on a cul-de-sac
lined with fake cacti
in Las Vegas,
or a gritty row house
with yellow evergreens
in Baltimore,
or a high-rise condominium
with a heart-shaped

swimming pool
in Albuquerque.
And when you discover
it's not at all
what you imagined,
the entire tableau begins
to vibrate, the very
molecules altering themselves
at high speed until
a new image appears,
conforming to your preconceptions,
which (it happens)
have also undergone
a subtle transformation,
and so in the end it's
only you who will change.

And this is something like
what I experienced
the first time I saw
a dead body lying in state,
my childhood neighbor Mrs. Luna,
whom I used to glimpse
daily in her flouncy robe
getting the mail
or paying the milkman
or watering her tiny lawn.
She was a recluse,
partial to Dixieland jazz,
with a smoky whiskey voice
and murky history;
twice widowed, a daughter
institutionalized,
a red De Soto convertible

parked by her house
on Sunday nights,
and a barking dog
that no one ever saw—
Mrs. Luna, whom I'd known
for years yet never
known at all,
there before me at age ten
and nothing like what I expected.

Jazz

When my mother was pregnant with me
she worked at a record company
that produced jazz
(jive jump swing & bebop)
and spent many afternoons
that summer and fall
at recording sessions
on the West Side of Manhattan
talking with the musicians between takes
sipping Coca-Cola
eating sandwiches with the engineers
closing her eyes
and tapping her feet to the music
and me there inside her
drums bass piano trumpet & trombone
and all those saxophones
working on my sensibilities
such as they were
like someone at the bottom of a swimming pool
who hears a band playing up above
under the moon on a warm night
taking it in
under the bigger bass of her heartbeat
all those rhythms
and crosscurrents of sound
(and moving to it?)
all those rhythms
I must have been listening for
months later when I was born
my ear cocked for them
in the loud world
and where were they?
all those rhythms

across from the gas station
a bus stopped every ten minutes
under the blue streetlight
and discharged a single passenger.
Never more than one.
A one-armed man with a cane.
A girl in red leather.
A security guard carrying his lunch box.
They stepped into the light,
looked left, then right, and disappeared.
Otherwise, the street was empty,
the wind off the river gusting paper and leaves.
Then the pay phone near the bus stop
started ringing; for five minutes it rang,
until another bus slid in
and a couple emerged,
their hats pulled down low.
The man walked up the street,
but the woman hesitated,
then answered the phone and stood
frozen with the receiver to her ear.
The man came back for her,
but she waved him away
and at the same moment her hat blew off
and skidded down the street.
The man followed it, holding his own hat,
and the woman began talking into the phone.
And she kept talking,
the wind tossing her hair wildly,
and the man never returned
and no more buses came after that.

In the Country

The lamplight, whirring
with mosquitoes, streams
out the screen door,
across the lawn,
and enters the forest.
Mist is rising from the ferns.
All the windows are open
and the wind is blowing
through the house,
over the meadow,
and rippling the surface
of the lake.
When your voice breaks
the stillness,
my pulse jumps—
as if I'm leaning
over the roof
of a tall building,
the full moon blazing
in my eyes.
One stormy night in Rome
I sat up for hours
with a woman I met
on the Paris express.
She, too, spoke with
that shivering cadence
in the blue darkness—
about her family in Spain,
her father the blind poet
and his whitewashed
house on a cliff
overlooking the sea.

In the morning
I opened my eyes
and she was crouched
at the foot of the bed
reciting his poems
from memory.
Years later, I heard
her father had been imprisoned
and her husband and son
had died of cholera;
committed to a sanitarium,
her hands and feet swollen
and her hair
falling out in sheaves—
dry as wheat—
she crept up to the roof
one night during a blizzard,
waited for the bells
to ring Vespers,
and jumped.

You've brought all this
back to me.
The thunder and lightning,
and the cats crying
like frightened angels
on the Via Cavour
while rain drilled the rooftops.
I tell myself it happened
a long time ago
and that here (miles
from the nearest road)
nothing can touch us,
even as moonlight crosses

the lake and the meadow
and enters the bedroom
window, enfolding you
like a sheet
and carrying you away.

Scarlet Lake

Derain, after his wife's
suicide, awoke in the Alps
in a small hotel.
The grass was crazy with bees—
and how the fish
were jumping on the lake!
He gazed over it for hours,
smoking his blunt meerschaum
with the amber stem.
A spider plant hung its
satellites around his head.
Embers hissed in the stove.
In the eggshell demitasse
the coffee grounds swirled
like ocean sediment,
glinting with lights.
He watched the fat cook
amble up through the pines
clutching a pair
of ducks the porter
had ambushed at dawn.
Their bright green feathers
were streaked with mud.
Blood speckled their bills.
When a storm swept in from
the west—from France—
the rain slanting down
hard across the mountains,
only the surface of the lake
remained undisturbed,
placid: very slowly
it turned a deep red.

Cancer Ward

The dark plant at the end
of the long corridor
has not been watered for days.
Light streaming through
the venetian blinds encircles
it with bands of dust.
A fly with one wing
hangs from the edge
of the topmost leaf.
Another fly is buzzing a zigzag
up and down the window,
ticking against the glass,
trying to get out.
Beyond a set of double doors,
around a corner,
a man is coughing violently.
Behind another door,
marked NO ADMITTANCE,
a machine is whirring
and a woman is crying.
A car horn sounds faintly
on the street below,
as if it is coming from
many miles at sea,
muffled by dense fog.
Like a ship returning
from those distant islands
where the dead lie shoulder to shoulder
in white sand
under a full moon.

The islands where thousands
of these plants grow
in endless, silent fields
and nothing—not even the black wind—
can ruffle their heavy leaves.

On the Peninsula

Lit from below, the blue water
flows to us on three sides.
Yellow crabs scuttle across the sand
and the moon sails over the mountains.
The stars are set close and bright—
it would take us a dozen human lifetimes,
traveling at the speed of light,
to reach the nearest one.
To reach the seafloor
takes less than a minute;
lungs straining, we glimpse
a million stars pinpointed
in the eyes of the fish,
schools of them hovering
in our torch beams
as the currents carry us from shore,
away from the rustling grass
and the deep orchard
and the house where our bodies,
locked fast, turn under a blue sheet.

Stars

The three *cantiche* of the *Divina Commedia*
close with the word *stelle*
because Dante wanted to emphasize
that the soul, in its long journey,
should aspire always to the highest state of nature.

Empedocles postulated that the energy
churning within stars also powered
the circuits of the human brain,
and that all animate matter on Earth,
at the moment of death, streamed a column
of luminous molecules upward into the heavens.

Poseidonius defined man as "the beholder
and expounder of heaven," his eyes, capable
of examining the remotest constellations,
marvels of nature, "tiny mirrors"
in which immensity is reflected inward.

From a muddy field in Buxton, North Carolina,
these same stars swirl into crescents—
vast wheels drawing us out of ourselves, it's true;
but tonight would we want to leave behind
this cold sea wind, these birds, this thumping
in our chests that echoes like a drumbeat
down to the soles of our feet, grounding us.

Approaching Antarctica

The slate sky is streaked
baby blue
and the sea,
smooth as a mirror,
reflects passing clouds.
The ship's titanium hull
hisses through the ice,
past islands of glass,
her nuclear engines
humming to the tune
of a billion atoms
splitting, spitting
forth electrons.
In the prow, a blind
man is clutching
a handful of cherries
while the terns,
crying harshly,
wheel overhead;
in the stern, three
men with binoculars
gaze at the horizon,
the jagged lightning bolts
and the squalls
wobbling like tops.
The satellite dish
a hundred feet up
is revolving slowly,
heaped with snow,
but still the messages
from the ionosphere,
from satellites

orbiting the Earth
at dizzying speed,
are crackling in,
informing us
of the dangers
we'll encounter tonight—
the icebergs, gale winds,
and treacherous currents—
when the ship, its
portholes glinting topaz,
parts the curtain
of a raging blizzard
and cuts through
miles of ice floes,
the snowflakes flashing
phosphorescent as
fallout, or fireflies,
or volcanic embers
blown south
from the equator,
which no longer seems
so far away;
as if the southern
hemisphere, bowl-shaped
(like one of those
paper models
used to illustrate
a theorem of geometry),
has been folded
over upon itself,
so that the equator
touches a single point:
the South Pole.

Ultimately, at either pole,
or in other places
of vast solitude—
like a small room
in the predawn—
you must keep
in mind Lucretius's
aside (while discussing
the movements of atoms)
that "all life is a
struggle in the dark."
And all men in their dreams
are wrestling their
opposite numbers—
clothed in the colors
of death—
struggling to survive,
to triumph,
and finally to vault
the four walls
of their perceptions
until they free-float
into the heady ether
of that famous sphere
which is everywhere
with a center
that is nowhere.

In the Year of the Comet

On the morning the comet
is to streak through
the Earth's atmosphere
for the first time
in thirty-eight years,
snow sifts from the low
clouds and the pigeons
huddle on icy ledges.
The people of the city
go about their business,
eating and drinking
and making money,
confessing to crimes
and confessing their love.
The comet last appeared
in the month I was born,
and in the intervening
years—while my life
has followed its own
erratic course—it has
traveled past Venus
and Mercury, around (and
dangerously close to)
the sun, and then out
beyond Pluto, its orbit
brushing the outer rim
of the solar system.
Now, because of the storm
blanketing this part
of North America,
I won't see it pass;
but standing by a window

with eyes closed, I still
hope to feel a tingle
in my nerve endings,
a hum of recognition
in my bloodstream,
a response of some sort
to the questions
circling in my head:
When the comet next
returns, (if I am not
dead) where will I be
as I approach eighty,
and what will I be
called on to remember
of my own life for
the benefit of others
and how much will I
have forgotten in order
to live with myself?
Will I even recall
this comet I never saw,
which hisses across
the sky at ten-forty-one
for less than a minute
before hurtling back
into space, toward the sun—
even more dangerously
close to the sun.

From 5° & OTHER POEMS (1995)

Hibiscus Tea

The cup of tea in the dying man's room trembled
with each blow of the laborer's hammer.
Across the road, by the dusty trees,
they were splitting stone in fierce sunlight.
The shadows of the men clotting

with the shadows of the trees;
the stone to be hewn for an aqueduct
that would relieve future droughts;
the tea, red as blood, gradually
overflowing the cup and filling its saucer.

And the man, dead before the sun sank
behind the broken teeth of the mountains,
confessing no sins and tasting blood on his lips
when he parted them for the last time
to complain of a sudden, deep thirst.

The Quiñero Sisters, 1968

Against the flares of falling stars
over the man-made lake
in the middle of which we were reclining
on a creaking raft, they sang a wicked
duet of "Be My Baby," swaying and dipping
in their identical white bikinis,
snapping their wrists like The Ronettes.
The water dripping from their hair.
They were twins who were not identical.
Victoria's eyes a deep blue.
Virginia's a pale brown.
(A genetic marvel, as I knew
from my biology texts.)
Virginia was a soprano.
Victoria, with her husky whisper, a contralto.
In the moonlight, their faces shone.
Lips gleaming. Teeth flashing like silver.
To our left, in the deep darkness,
the waterfall roared; one night in June
a rowboat had strayed over those falls
and two friends of ours were drowned,
their naked bodies, tightly embraced,
dredged up the next morning a mile downriver.
Now, on the last night of the summer,
we had come in a borrowed, baby-blue
convertible, driving fast along the mountain
roads, the high-beam lights picking up
the red eyes of animals crouched
in the grass—Victoria, Virginia,
her boyfriend, who was also named Nick,
and me, behind the wheel. The other Nick
was about to go to Vietnam, and I was

about to enter college, and side by side
on the raft we were passing a bottle
of red wine while the girls sang.
We were seventeen, except for Nick,
a carpenter's apprentice, who had turned
eighteen in July and been drafted in August.
And five months later, in a library in
Cambridge in dead of winter, I would see
his name listed among the dead in a newspaper—
killed in action outside Da Nang.
But that night, under the sky riddled
with stars, with the wind licking our lips
and the water lapping softly beneath
the raft, he and I (two boys with the same
name) never took our eyes off the Quiñero
sisters (twins who didn't even look
like sisters), revolving their open
palms in rhythmical circles, as if
they were trying to erase the night.
Oh, since the day I saw you,
I have been waiting for you,
You know I will adore you, till Eternity
They harmonized in and around the melody,
until, hands on hips and hair flying,
they threw their heads back and held
the last sweet note. And held it. For hours,
it seemed, while the moon slid through
the clouds, and the bats skimmed the water,
and the fish jumped, and then, reluctantly,
we left that raft, moored to the muddy lake
bottom, and two by two swam back to shore.
Virginia and Nick hurried up the hill,
and Victoria and I laid a blanket under
the trees, on the grass bank, and peeled off

our suits. Shuddering now, with the insects
buzzing around us like static, she opened
her arms and pulled me on top of her.
Ten years later, after two busted marriages,
her sister would open her wrists
and slip into a tub of blood-warm water.
And a year after that, to the day, Victoria
would be killed in a car crash, beside
a man she met at a party, who crossed
the double line into oncoming traffic
with a bottle cradled between his knees.
But when I held her that night,
breathing in the scent of her hair,
I felt her fingers dance along my spine
and her eyelashes moisten as she whispered
in my ear—I can hear it clearly—
her voice even then falling away from me,
"Be my baby now . . ."

Terminus

Here is a piece of required reading
at the end of our century
the end of a millennium that began with the crusades

The transcript of an interview
between a Red Cross doctor
and a Muslim girl in Bosnia
twelve years old
who described her rape by men
calling themselves soldiers
different men every night one after the other
six seven eight of them
for a week
while she was chained by the neck
to a bed in her former schoolhouse
where she saw her parents and her brothers
have their throats slit and tongues cut out
where her sister-in-law
nineteen years old and nursing her baby
was also raped night after night
until she dared to beg for water
because her milk had run dry
at which point one of the men
tore the child from her arms
and as if he were "cutting an ear of corn"
(the girl's words)
lopped off the child's head
with a hunting knife
tossed it into the mother's lap
and raped the girl again
slapping her face
smearing it with her nephew's blood

and then shot the mother
who had begun to shriek
with the head wide-eyed in her lap
shoving the gun into her mouth
and firing twice

All of this recounted to the doctor
in a monotone
a near whisper in a tent
beside an icy river
where the girl had turned up frostbitten
wearing only a soiled slip
her hair yanked out
her teeth broken

All the history you've ever read
tells you this is what men do
this is only a sliver of the reflection
of the beast
who is a fixture of human history
and the places you heard of as a boy
that were his latest stalking grounds
Auschwitz Dachau Treblinka
and the names of their dead
and their numberless dead whose names have vanished
each day now find their rolls swelled
with kindred souls
new names new numbers
from towns and villages
that have been scorched from the map

1993 may as well be 1943
and it should be clear now
that the beast in his many guises
the flags and vestments

in which he wraps himself
and the elaborate titles he assumes
can never be outrun

As that girl with the broken teeth
loaded into an ambulance
strapped down on a stretcher
so she wouldn't claw her own face
will never outrun him
no matter where she goes
solitary or lost in a crowd
the line she follows
however straight or crooked
will always lead her back to that room
like the chamber at the bottom
of Hell in the Koran
where the Zaqqūm tree grows
watered by scalding rains
"bearing fruit like devils' heads"

In not giving her name
someone has noted at the end
of the transcript that the girl herself
could not or would not recall it
and then describes her as a survivor

Which of course is from the Latin
meaning to live on
to outlive others

I would not have used that word

The Skeleton of a Trout in Shallow Water

wedged between two stones
near the bank of a rushing stream
startled the old man with the shock
of white hair who uncovered it
while stooping to pick watercress.
For a long time he examined the skeleton—
skull, ribs, and spine polished clean—
before dislodging it with his cane
and watching it spin away
into the fast current
and disappear through the shadows
of the overhanging trees.
Then, with the sun beating down
on his head and bleaching
the fields that stretched away
to the mountains, he released
the dripping clump of watercress
he had been clutching all that time
and watched it float away, too,
dark and tangled in the clear water.

When the Hurricane Swerved Toward the Island

a radio began playing through the forest
where it was always night
and the thin trunks of the bamboo trees
clicked together like hundreds of clocks ticking

There were no houses beyond that forest
just the burned-out church
in which the high grass glowed like moonlight
and ghosts lined the broken pews sipping darkness

And beyond the church miles of scorched sugarcane
and fields of jagged boulders
and hidden valleys to which the tropicbirds descended
from the mountains without once beating their wings

Until that moment on my terrace overlooking the bay
many sounds had drifted from the forest
the squawking of toucans and the cries of the cats
and the insects' staccato clatter but never a radio

And now it drowned out everything else
first with a snatch of music which kept changing keys
and then a voice swimming in static and not altogether human
that tried to reach us from across the sea

After a Long Illness

A man lighter than air enters
the glass house, switches on
every lamp, and turns the radio
to a station broadcasting
the sound of birds' wings flapping
skyward over a deep lake at dawn.

He pours himself a glass of water
from a tall pitcher on which
a crane, drinking from a pitcher,
has been etched in the enamel.
He makes a sandwich of brightly colored
pieces of paper and slices it in half.

Opening a window, he reels in
a clothesline with two billowing
sheets, white as ocean clouds,
and lays them on a bed so high
he would need a ladder to reach it
were he not lighter than air.

He reclines on the bed with a book
of photographs of birds in flight
and gazes up through the glass roof
at the full moon and the stars.
In the morning, a quart of milk
is left at the door, a letter is

dropped through the mail slot,
the lawn is mowed and the shrubs
trimmed, but there is no one home.
A woman arrives in a see-through
raincoat, switches off the lamps
and the radio, climbs to the roof,

and lets out a kite on a long string.
Winding the string in hours later,
she finds it attached, not to the kite,
but to a man who is fast asleep,
trailing vapors, his arms folded
across his chest like wings.

A Storm

It's raining cats and dogs.
And did you know that "vindaloo" (as in
Shrimp Vindaloo) is not an Indian word at all,
but a pidgin slurring of the Portuguese
for "wine of garlic"?

There is a film I have otherwise forgotten
(but not the makeshift cinema in which I viewed it:
a converted bakery storeroom on the island of Spetses)
that ended with the line:
"If no one escaped drowning, who are these strangers?"

What we will never know,
watching this cold sky turn on its invisible axis,
is how much punishment you have absorbed—
you, the victim of crimes, and you, the criminal—
for a set of principles no one can remember.

The rain on our lips is fiery with spices.
We are hurrying along a tangle of slick streets,
up blind alleys and through hidden archways,
the wind whipping our coats,
to an appointment we should not keep.
The words on the scrap of paper crumpled in your hand
    confirm this.

Before the night began to run like ink,
engulfing everyone who had no place to hide,
a woman with a beautiful voice was cooking for us
without questions or reservations
in a kitchen that glowed orange.

In that film, it was just such a voice—
but frightened—that delivered the last line.

Also in a city whose streets had no end.
Also while rats scratched about in the darkness,
as in the bakery's storeroom.

Still searching for crumbs where there could be none.
The story of someone else's life
which nevertheless must infringe on our own,
until it furiously alters the facts we had stored up
and polished for so many years.

On that scrap of paper is also a telephone number
you misdialed, which has sent us off in the wrong direction.
Something an impartial observer, watching us zigzag,
might ascribe to fate before growing nervous
and asking someone at the edge of the crowd,
"If no one escaped drowning, who are these strangers?"

Assignation After Attending a Funeral

A clear spring night
and the wind is filling my shirt,
rushing in the sleeves
and encircling me
as a bat glides over the steeple
where the clock lit up bright green
has no hands, no face.

The Palm Reader

In her storefront living room—
overstuffed couch, oversized TV, a bowl of mints
on the Plexiglas coffee table—
she watches *Edge of Night* and files her nails.
The paraphernalia pertaining to her trade
crowd a shelf beneath the large green hand
painted onto the window: a tarot deck,
coins and obelisks, a chalky bust with numbered
phrenological divisions on the skull.
Through the beaded curtain in the rear
some clues emerge as to *her* life:
two children trading insults,
a man calling out, "Eggs!"
as a frying pan clatters into a sink,
a dog running by with a wig in his mouth.
She herself is plump, heavily made up,
wearing a red dress and a shawl imprinted
with the signs of the zodiac.
A gold pyramid hangs from her throat
and she has combed glittering
silver stars through her black hair.
From a plush rocker she beckons you,
at the window, to a straight-back chair
in which she will divine (according to the sign
on the door) "the roads into your future,
and helpful information from the Beyond."
Though the latter, especially, tempts
you powerfully, you decline,
and she shrugs with a rueful smile.
And because it is close to noon,
and the sidewalk is empty, as you cross
the street she closes up for lunch.

Her living room in which matters of life
and death—of human destiny laid bare—
suddenly reverts to its other function:
husband slumped on the couch clutching a beer,
children sopping bread across paper plates,
the dog sprawled under the table.
All of them watching *Edge of Night* now.
The fate of whose characters, which keeps
a faithful public tuning in day after day,
year after year, is presumably known
to this woman, lighting a cigarette
and surveying that room, open to all passersby
yet utterly remote, as inescapable
as the future itself, that jumps out
at her from every stranger's hand.

Hanalei Valley

A solitary horse is grazing in grass
that reaches to his shoulders.
A white egret is perched on his back,
reflected in the river that flows
past them without a ripple.
Enormous clouds span the sky.
In the deep stillness it seems as if the earth
has stopped rotating on its axis.
Then the egret takes flight,
rising in a long arc with its slow-beating wings
against the lush, green mountains
where it rains day and night,
where it is raining even now
as I write this,
as you read it.

from 5°

#1

Down the long avenues the north wind
doubles over the strongest men.

Everything has turned to iron:
buildings, pavement, the stunted trees.

Even the sky, from which lapis stars glint,
painful to the naked eye.

But for the clouds of their breath,
a man and his dog might be statues.

The pretzel vendor, his fingers brittle,
rakes his coals and sucks on a chip of ice.

In an archway, under a slanting hat,
a young woman is lighting a cigarette.

There is nothing in her eyes but the spit
of flame—amber enclosing a crimson thread—

as her shadow slips away, into a waiting car,
and the sidewalk swallows her up.

The smoke of her cigarette lingers,
coiling and floating across the street

intact—a halo that hovers all night
beneath the parapet of the church

where the angel with feverish eyes
snatches it up at dawn as the snow

begins to fall, and places it—heavy
as marble suddenly—behind his head.

In a letter to his brother Theo,
van Gogh wrote that he had earlier
that morning received the greatest
compliment ever paid him—by a doctor
who, upon examining him, remarked:
"I suppose you are an ironworker."
Van Gogh also mentioned that while in England
he applied for the position of "Evangelist
among the miners in the coal mines,
but they turned me down . . ."

Coal and iron: the guts of the Earth,
scraped forth for furnaces and fires.
Brazil took its name from a redwood
whose bark reminded the conquistadors
of burning coals (braise in Portuguese).
How would van Gogh have painted in Brazil?
The choppy tropical colors slashing
the hills that rise up from the sea.
How would he have painted this street,
so cold the beams of headlights from cars
that passed hours ago remain frozen in midair.

Displayed in the coin shop window
below the Spanish doubloons and Flemish guilders,
in a row of talismans on felt cushions,
a gold disc deflects a ray of moonlight.

The sea-green card beneath it reads:
DISC EMPLOYED BY JOHN DEE (1527–1608)
WHO TRIED TO LEARN THE SECRETS
OF NATURE FROM ANGELS.

This same John Dee, court mathematician,
was a close friend to Sir Walter Ralegh
and Thomas Harriot, the first man
to map the lunar surface with a telescope.

The language Dee invented for communicating
with angels he called "Enochian."
His partner, Edward Kelley, was a medium
and a forger, whose ears had been lopped off.

Coins of the realm were Kelley's specialty.
Later, he was murdered in prison.
Dee died impoverished, reduced to casting
horoscopes in a provincial town.

He was reputed to be the model for Prospero.
His gold disc is ringed with concentric circles.
A sun at its center; a cross; four stone arches.
And hieroglyphics that hold the key
to what he learned from the angels,
which he never shared with anyone.

Beneath the thick ice and the gray waters
of the lake there are seven inches
in which a man can breathe. So long as
he can tread water while tilting his head
upward at a forty-five degree angle
indefinitely—until he freezes to death.

Harry Houdini, in Chicago to expose a pair
of bogus mediums, took time out
to have himself submerged in Lake Michigan
straitjacketed and weighted with chains
inside a padlocked, cast-iron milk container.
He escaped his restraints in thirty seconds,
but then could not locate the opening
that had been sawed in the ice for him;
and for two hours, wearing only a bathing
suit, he paddled slowly, searching
for the way out of that water cold
enough to kill a man in ten minutes.

When he emerged without physical injury,
not even frostbite, he attributed it
to his "mastery of all bodily controls."
Then he returned to his hotel suite,
and after dinner took a very hot bath,
followed by a very cold one—as was his custom.

A man with a telescope on a marble runway
is shielding his eyes from the moon.
Like a match head, the Dog Star flares

over the island, famous for its cornfields
and its quarry: white marble so plentiful
it is used in lieu of concrete for everything

from the floors and stairways of the humblest
homes to this runway, hewn by a team of masons
and laid in place by farmers and fishermen

who wanted an air connection to the mainland.
Instead, the next year, they got the *Luftwaffe*,
first dropping paratroopers and then landing

transport planes with wings dusted by snow
crossing the Alps. For two years the Nazis
terrorized the island with armored cars,

flamethrowers, and attack dogs with iron teeth.
They built torture chambers in the town hall,
dynamited the church, and lopped off the mayor's ears.

They executed half the young men and flew
the other half to Germany in dead of night.
When Allied warships appeared on the horizon

one morning, the Nazis fled by air and were
shot down over the sea. Survivors washed up
in the surf and the same farmers and fishermen

clubbed them to death with oars and shovels.
A salt-streaked obelisk marks the site,
with the names of the islanders murdered

during the occupation carved into its marble.
Meanwhile, the man with the telescope (the former
mayor, deaf and dumb, with a woolen cap

covering the stubs of his ears) is still
waiting for the plane to arrive bearing
the film company that plans to shoot *The Tempest*

on location. The actor who will play Prospero,
still learning his lines, glances through
the window at the island, so flooded

with moonlight it seems to lie underwater,
that whiter-than-white runway shining like a beacon,
as it once shone for the Germans, who in Berlin,

where *The Merchant of Venice* was performed nightly,
flung copies of *The Tempest* into their bonfires
while the dogs, in packs, barked from the rooftops.

"Iron occurs native in meteorites" (according to
the dictionary) "and is vital to biological processes."
Brought to the bloodstream from the farthest reaches

of the solar system. Only in meteorites is iron
found uncombined with other elements.
Tonight a meteor shower streams out of the chaotic

glitter of the stars. When stray dogs congregate
on the rooftops of abandoned tenements, the yellow
moon casts their shadows for an entire city block.

In ancient Egypt, Anubis, the dog-headed god, led
souls down a torchlit stairway to the underworld
and wore beads of meteoric iron around his neck.

Iron coins were placed under the tongues of the dead
in Crete to pay the stone-eyed ferryman Charon
for passage across the River Styx. In Rome, too,

where all gems and minerals beneath the earth's
surface were, by law, the property of Pluto,
god of the dead: iron and coal, opal and lapis.

Then, as now, grave robbers preferred aboveground
mausoleums: no digging; just a padlock to pick
and a casket to pry open. After which, shunning

the coin within its cage of clamped teeth,
they slipped bracelets and rings from skeletal hands
that shared a single trace element with meteorites:

iron, forged in the icy furnaces beyond Pluto—
beyond the Dog Star—where darkness is no longer
visible, and even the gods of the dead fear to go.

#13

In 1910 Houdini was the first man to fly
an airplane successfully in Australia.
It was a biplane, purchased in France,
which he took to Melbourne on a ship.
During the two-week voyage,
he was continually seasick,
yet spent hours in the cargo hold,
poised at the controls of his plane.
He had HOUDINI painted on the fuselage
and wings in red and gold.

In Melbourne he gave two performances nightly.
He made a full-grown elephant disappear.
He caused a man's top hat to fill with coins.
He had himself submerged, straitjacketed
and handcuffed, in a tank of ice water.
Then he left his wife at their hotel and hurried
to a desert airstrip to sit in his plane.
He kept this up for weeks, studying charts,
waiting for the weather to clear.

On the evening of February 18th, a crowd
watched him leap manacled from Queen's Bridge
into the muddy waters of the Yarra River.
Moments later, a dead man floated to the surface.
The onlookers panicked, and when Houdini
reappeared, he was so startled to see
the corpse that he nearly drowned,
and had to be hauled
into a rowboat by his attendants.

Finally, on March 16th, under cloudless skies,
he took off in his plane, circled, and landed.

He completed three flights that day,
covering seven miles at an altitude of ninety feet.
At each stop, bigger crowds cheered him on.
In April, he made four more flights
before crashing outside Sydney on the 22nd.
He walked away from the wreckage unscathed
and told his wife he had not slept in a month.

"I now seem to have lost the habit," he added.
To his journal he confided that history
would remember him, not as a magician,
but an aviation pioneer.
During the voyage home, he was seasick.
He never flew again.

An angel is signing his name in blue light
on a black wall. Recording his history,
over thirteen centuries, on the head of a pin.
Writing in a language known only to other angels,
but with such variations as to confuse even them.

The fragments that will survive are being spirited
away by fugitive translators who will languish
in underground prisons until they die.

In the courtyard of one such prison,
modeled after the innermost circle of Dante's
Inferno, a statue of a frozen, bearded man

is planted headfirst in the ice, like Satan
who is to remain in this position for all
eternity after being hurled down from Heaven.

He has three faces, six eyes, and three mouths
from which dark blood issues. For recreation,
the prisoners are allowed to climb in his beard.

In London, Newgate Prison was rebuilt in 1780,
following the blueprint of a fantastical drawing
by Piranesi, executed thirty years earlier.

Another instance of life imitating art,
which, contrary to popular misconceptions,
is not the exception but the rule.

As van Gogh knew, in his final days at Arles,
moving into a house called the "Yellow House"
when he began painting in yellow.

And Shakespeare, who understood that the hard
facts he pillaged from Plutarch were prefigured
in myths—the wellspring of history—

which is why the *Parallel Lives* begins
(apologetically) with Theseus and Romulus,
founders of Athens and Rome in those remote ages

of "prodigies and fables, the province of poets."
The stuff the angels have transcribed for us.
only a fraction of which—like the number
of waking moments a prisoner actually forgets
he is imprisoned—will be deciphered.

On the other side of the world,
as on the other side of a dream,
the surface of the Sahara Desert is 140°.

In the fourth book of his *Histories*
Herodotus catalogs the tribes who inhabited
"the great belt of sand beyond the regions

where wild beasts are found," including
the Psylli, who declared war on the south wind
(after it dried up their water supply)

and, marching all night, were buried alive
in sand by the wind; and the Atarantes,
"the only people in the world to do without names,"

who screeched and heaped curses
upon the sun as it rose, trailing ashes
on the horizon. Other tribes he mentions

are the Maxyes, "dog-headed men" who dyed
their bodies red; and the Gyzantes,
who did the same, and ate flying snakes

and monkeys, and also perfected a way
to make honey without bees; and off the desert
coast, on an island called Cyrauis, a tribe

of women who lived by a lake "and dipped
feathers smeared with pitch into the muddy
lake bottom and brought up gold dust"

which they sprinkled on their hair
before going into battle or making love.
These tribes shared the same god.

From a vast underworld he commanded legions
of ants in silver armor whose sole task
was to fetch him the dead; in a single night

they could break down and transport
an entire body through their tunnels.
The god himself was transparent, composed

of a substance from the other side of the world,
so cold it could tear the skin from a man's flesh.
Ice:

when the god opened his arms at dawn
to welcome the dead, it melted into
a swift, deep river and carried them away.

John Davis, explorer and navigator, died the night
The Tempest was first performed in London.
As a young man, he sailed deep into the polar

regions, along uncharted sea lanes, on the bark
Moonlight, in search of the Northwest Passage.
Near the Arctic Circle, he saw a mountain

of gold on a distant headland, which he named
Mount Raleigh, after his friend Sir Walter,
whose obsession with El Dorado, the elusive

city of gold in the Amazon jungle, was well known.
But Davis's concerns were with iron, not gold.
He recorded that the people he encountered

slept on their feet, were left-handed,
and (like the white-eyed dogs that pulled
their sleds) able to see for miles in the darkness.

Also, that they craved all things iron—
hooks, knives, buttons, anchors—
which they were not above stealing openly.

Their word for iron, he added, was *Aoh.*
Davis befriended these people, but thought
them "witches," capable of "many enchantments,"

including their ability to kindle fires
in howling wind and to remain neck-deep in icy
waters, "amongst the fishes," for whole days.

He wondered at their diet, for "they consume all
their meat raw, and live most upon fish, and drink
salt water, and eat grass and ice with delight."

Continuing northward, Davis encountered an iceberg
so huge ("with bays and capes and high cliffs")
that it took him two weeks to sail past it.

Then a mysterious illness spread among his men:
overnight, their hair turned white and, scalded
by fever, they lost all desire for sleep.

Violent storms and high seas racked the ship.
Those who didn't drown, or freeze to death,
took their own lives. Davis survived, and with a skeleton

crew pushed on through sheets of blinding snow.
Months later, when they brought the *Moonlight*
back to Portsmouth, he remained on board, alone,

and in the darkness of his cabin made his final
entry in the ship's log, writing in a clear hand
that he had dropped anchor in Iceland, and Greenland,

and then a country no European had ever laid eyes on,
whose coordinates he noted carefully.
He called it Desolation.

In October, 1888, Paul Gauguin joined van Gogh
in the Yellow House at Arles and dreamt
of the desert after sketching the flora of Martinique
on a tablecloth for his companion after dinner.

For six nights he had the same dream, and on
the seventh woke to find van Gogh standing,
fast asleep, beside his bed with a pistol.
The next morning, Gauguin executed his first

canvas in that house: two girls picking
mangoes near a stream, under the gaze
of a red horse tethered to a banyan tree.
A single element of his recurrent dream

appeared in the lower left-hand corner
of this painting, beneath the dipping arm
of a lush fern: a shiny, long-legged insect
unknown in those days, but identifiable now

as the Saharan silver ant. In his dream
hundreds of them were marching in lockstep
on the scorching sand, just as the Nazis'
armored legions would one day cross North Africa.

Gauguin's posthumous admirers naturally
thought the ant to be of a tropical species.
Gauguin himself, who had never visited
the desert, nearly painted over the ant,

he confided to his journal, until van Gogh
casually mentioned that he, too, had once
encountered such an insect in a dream.
Set not in the tropics, or the desert,

but in a kind of hell beneath that very house,
down steep steps, where men chained to a wall
under hot lamps screamed while silver-helmeted
(antlike) soldiers lacerated their backs.

During the occupation, the Yellow House
would serve as headquarters for the Gestapo
in Arles, and it was in the basement
that they conducted their interrogations.

"Leave the ant in," van Gogh advised, fifty-two
years earlier, "as the emissary to your paradise
from the inferno we call Europe." And Gauguin did.

The Hyperboreans—"people beyond the North Wind"—
according to Diodorus Siculus inhabited an island
from which the moon "appears to be but a little
distance from the earth and to have upon it
prominences, like those of the earth," easily visible.

Some believed this island to be England, home
of Thomas Harriot, the first lunar cartographer,
and botanist to Ralegh's Virginia expedition
in 1586, two thousand years after the Hyperboreans
disappeared from the annals of history.

Herodotus mentions a tribe even farther north,
of one-eyed men and griffons who guard hoards
of gold in ice fortresses and "make war upon the ice"
during their long winters when "the ground is frozen
iron hard," requiring, not water, but fire to soften it.

Long before John Davis plied Arctic waters,
word had reached these two Greek historians,
who had never ventured north of the Black Sea,
that there was such a people, skilled in fishing through ice
and hunting in darkness, who slept on their feet.

The snow in that place was so thick, Herodotus reported,
that it resembled an "unceasing wind filled
with feathers"; while Diodorus referred to it
as a "great cloud shredded by the North Wind."
It was another Englishman, Sir Thomas Browne,

born when Davis and Harriot were old men,
who chose for his meditation on death

and the underworld, *Hydriotaphia, Urne-Buriall*
(filled with digressions on astral nomenclature,
the psychology of arches and obelisks,

and the fact that Roman colonists in Britain,
when they left off torturing and dispossessing
the resident Saxons, taught them the art
of minting coins), a fittingly Hyperborean epigraph,
icy in its simplicity, by yet another citizen

of the sunny south: the line of verse Sextus
Propertius, in 15 B.C., had etched onto the urn
that would hold his ashes—white as snow—
in the catacombs of Rome,
"See, I am now what can be lifted with five fingers."

The polestar (Polaris) during the Dark Ages
was called the "Nail of the Heavens"—
an iron nail hammered into the frozen sky.

Between this nail and the center of the Underworld—
an onyx cave whose domed ceiling was spiked
with stars—was stretched the *axis mundi,* like a harp
string, sounding the solitary note of Creation.

Only a single piece of land lay along this axis:
an island of iron boulders from which St. Brendan
the Voyager set sail for America a century

before Columbus, but ended up exploring
the Canary Islands with his party of monks,
who spoke in tongues and traded the native
inhabitants iron pebbles for ripe pomegranates.

In demonstrating the wonders of his faith,
St. Brendan caused a waterfall to flow upward,
and—like Prospero—called forth dead men

from their graves and darkened the sun at noon.
(Could it have been St. Brendan, rather than
John Dee or Walter Ralegh, who was the first,
most prodigious, model for Prospero?)

The number of his conversions remains cloudy,
but we know that one of his monks bolted
and remained behind on the westernmost island

of Hierro (Iron), hiding in a cave, living on
spiders, lizards, and the juice of sea grapes,
a Caliban crouched behind a curtain of foliage
who, watching his shipmates set sail for Ireland,

heard a single plucked note reverberating
in his ears. And when the rough sea was empty—
the breakers streaming a spray of gems off the rocks—

he crawled down to the beach and rolled in sand
black as coal and howled at that one star
nailed fast among a million wavering lights.

The *Voyager 2* satellite, launched from Florida
on a starry night in 1977 atop a booster rocket
propelled by liquid nitrogen (optimum temperature

at combustion: 5°), tonight sailed past Pluto
and its lone moon, Charon—named after
the ferryman who, with Cerberus the 3-headed dog,

is gatekeeper to the underworld—
leaving our solar system behind. It was
the *Voyager* that transmitted the first close-up

photographs of Saturn and Neptune, and then
Uranus and two of its icy moons, Ariel
and Miranda, which it had taken the satellite

fifteen years to reach. In 1957 the Russians
launched *Sputnik II* from Star City (a space
center erected on the Siberian permafrost)

with a single occupant, the dog Laika, a mixed
breed from Central Asia who was in his prime—
highly intelligent, good-natured, and trusting

to a fault. And after he had told them
(electrodes attached to his body and sensors
implanted in his brain) all they wanted

to know about weightlessness, motion sickness,
and the effects of gamma rays on a mammal
above the protection of the ozone layer,

they allowed him to spin out of the ionosphere
and hurtle toward the outer planets, where he died
a slow death when his supply of food,

water, and air ran out. Perfectly preserved
in the vacuum of his iron compartment,
Laika also flew past Ariel and Miranda,

past Pluto and Charon, into interstellar
space, where if he continues traveling
at his last recorded speed for 10,000 years—

at which time the tilt of the Earth's axis
will have shifted 5°, plunging it into
another Ice Age—Laika will reach Sirius,

the Dog Star, whose sapphire rays,
pinpointed in his black eyes, will enter
his body and flood it with light.

"Iron" in Sumerian means "metal from heaven."

The iron comprising 5% of the earth's crust
arrived here as meteors during the Ice Age.
When the iron core of a neutron star—

a steely sphere with a smooth surface—
collapses, it sounds a tremendous clang,
like a cymbal a thousand times the size

of the Sun, and rolls a sonic wave through
deep space, followed by a stream (as from
a cornucopia) of gold, silver, tin, and iron—

millions of tons of these metals buckshotting
into the cosmos while the former star flattens
into a black hole. The particle spray off

a single iron pellet of this buckshot may
after many years' travel enter our atmosphere
as a meteor shower, leveler of mountains

and cities, feared by ancient man, who,
regardless of the gods he worshipped,
always kept one eye trained on the heavens.

There was, in fact, a city named Iron (cited in
the Book of Joshua) in the mountains of northern
Palestine that disappeared without a trace.

Iron, with a hard *r,* is the Hebrew word for "fear."

Of the eighteen cities called Alexandria that Alexander
the Great founded or renamed, from the Sahara Desert
to the Arctic Circle, only the first, in Egypt, remains
standing after two millennia. According to Plutarch,

after Alexander proclaimed himself pharaoh,
he personally chose the site of the city, overruling
his architects, because of a dream in which an old
man directed him to the windy headland at the Nile

delta opposite the island of Pharos. The Arab
historian Mas'ūdī, insisting that the new pharaoh
was also a magician, reports that when the city's
foundations were being laid, "savage monsters" emerged

from the sea at night and tore down everything
that had been built by day. No watchmen, not even
crack troops posted on the beach, could deter them.
So Alexander had a box constructed, casket-shaped,

with sheets of glass on three sides, in which he
stretched out with paper and stylus. Weighted
with iron, the box was lowered to the seafloor,
where Alexander observed the monsters, who had

human torsos and the heads of beasts. After sketching
them, he ordered his sculptors to produce exact
likenesses in marble and position them along the shore.
When the sea monsters next appeared, and confronted

their own graven images, they plunged terrified back
into the sea and were never seen again. Mas'ūdī also
relates Alexander's little known exploits as an aviator,
explaining that when he traveled into the far north

Alexander built a "flying machine" in order to avoid
the icebound seas: a pair of griffons was chained to
a basket in which Alexander sat, raising a piece of meat
on a stick above their heads, inducing them to flight.

Pausanias notes that the icy water of the Styx, capable of
"dissolving glass and crystal, silver and gold,"
can only be contained by a mule's hoof.
Which is reputedly how it was served up

to Alexander during his fatal drinking bout in Babylon.
He was embalmed by Egyptian members of his court,
who spent twelve years building a proper chariot—
temple-sized, adorned with golden griffons—

to carry his body to Alexandria, where it was
placed in the same glass casket in which
he had been submerged to sketch the sea monsters.
And there he lay, a coin minted with his own image

under his tongue, on display for three hundred years.
Until his casket disappeared in the bustling city
which had sprung from his dreams, on a night so cold
blocks of ice were seen floating on the Nile.

Refracted by frozen clouds, the moon's
rays sweep the granite towers
and deflect off their black windows.
Behind each square of thick glass
a body reclines in sleep,
deaf to the wind-rattled streets.

Hesiod writes that the north wind makes
"the old man bend, round-shouldered as a wheel,"
and slicks the ice under his feet.
Stone Age men, grinding pigments from cobalt,
painted themselves, dog-headed, electric,
on stalactites in their caves.

In *The Book of Jubilees,* a heretical version
of Genesis flung into bonfires in the Dark Ages,
an Angel of Ice is mentioned, but not named.
Whereas Gabriel, the Angel of the North,
is one of only two angels named—
and praised—in the Old Testament.

He is said to preside over Paradise,
and to have leveled Sodom and Gomorrah.
Mohammed wrote that Gabriel "of the 140 pairs of wings"
dictated the Koran to him, *sura* by *sura.*
And Luke (1:26) credits him, not the Holy Ghost,
with begetting Jesus upon the Virgin Mary.

When Gabriel descends from the north,
with his staff of ice that extends
from the polestar to the center of the earth,
the frigid wind howls from his lips,
whipped up by his beating wings,
and doubles over the strongest men.

From THE CREATION OF
THE NIGHT SKY (1998)

Midsummer

Bashō says the body is composed of one hundred bones
   and nine openings.
Within which flimsy structure the spirit dwells.

Floating by the park at dusk, through the heavy trees,
the white building glides like a ship.

An amber lamp is lit in a top-floor window
and a woman in her robe is leaning on the sill, eyes closed
   to the sunset.

A violet shadow is pouring down the side of the building
   from her long hair.
Two pigeons are perched in the next window, against a
   black room.

Beyond the trees, down a rough slope, the river is winding
around the island, flowing into the sea.

Slowly the mist off the river coils around the building,
   concealing it.
And just as slowly it lifts.

Only now the woman's lamp is extinguished.
Her window remains open, the curtain flutters,

but there is no sign of her, laid down to sleep in the darkness—
her pale body with its one hundred bones and nine openings

from which the spirit will one day slip, like the mist seeping
back through the trees, along the river, out to sea.

X Rays

A door creaks open
a few inches
and light the blue of the sea
streams in from far away
from beyond the sea

dividing this empty room
with its four sealed windows
one in each wall
and its floorboards
like bars of iron glowing

A woman with a skeleton on fire
a man in whose stomach
goldfish orbit a star
a boy who's swallowed buffalo nickels
a girl with an extra rib

come and go over the years
as well as those unfortunates
who enter supine
with cracked skulls or blotched lungs
their hearts fluttering to a standstill

while that familiar pair
the reticent man in black
the wispy woman in white
who brought you into this world
and will usher you out of it

work the machinery
in close conjunction and silence
from behind the door
their shadows flowing down the long corridor
out the window into the night

Antiquities

The hands of Franz Liszt were painted
in pale green on the battered armoire
in a storefront before which sand was sprinkled
and a pyramidal sign read ANTIQUITIES—
objects many centuries older than antiques.

Yet nothing in that store dated back
to ancient Greece or Rome, to Egypt,
Assyria, or the Ch'in dynasty.
The oldest item was a set of cutlery
in a walnut case stamped *1899*.

It was February and sleet was falling
on a sharp diagonal onto Second Avenue.
The wind skidded a black hat through the traffic.
A bell tinkled when I entered the store,
and removing my gloves, examined the armoire.

There was no one behind the counter,
just a beaded curtain leading into darkness
from which suddenly the stormy concluding
chords of Liszt's second Hungarian
Rhapsody echoed, as if they had traveled

through a succession of rooms,
down untold, twisting corridors—
like the labyrinth in the bowels of a pyramid.
To play those chords properly, a pianist
must possess Liszt's two-octave reach,

accurately rendered in the green hands
poised over their keyboard,
which I reached out to touch as the wind
blew open the door and rushed in,
extending that long final chord indefinitely.

Jupiter Place, 1955

The three sisters who lived in the house surrounded
by hedges elaborately set a redwood table in their backyard:
twelve miniature cups and saucers, plates, spoons, and forks,
on a white paper tablecloth the wind, at any moment,
threatened to lift skyward, where it would crumple,
then billow, indistinguishable from the clouds.
I had often wondered what went on behind those hedges
down the street: I knew the girls were twice my age—
I was four—and that I was the youngest
of the nine guests invited to their tea party;
the only other boy, around six, was someone
I had never seen before on our street.
He had hair pomaded so flat it shone like a mirror,
and on his starched collar he wore a clip-on bow tie.
"He's our cousin from Syracuse," the eldest sister informed me,
and, seated beside me, he didn't speak to anyone.
I had never heard of Syracuse, and even now I do not know
if he had journeyed from upstate New York or the coast of
    Sicily.
Expecting cake, I was served crab apples, acorns, and a
    pinecone,
and from the teapot an imaginary arc of "Darjeeling"—
the word rolled off the second sister's tongue—
filled my cup to the brim before she offered me
first a sugar bowl without sugar, then a pitcher and a yellow
    dish,
murmuring, "Cream or lemon," at which point, vastly
disappointed but getting the hang of things, I took an
    imaginary
wedge of lemon, squeezed it into my cup, and refrained
from biting into the one edible prop, my crab apple.
Then I noticed that the youngest sister had wandered

across the lawn and was dancing under an enormous
weeping willow, up high on her toes—
the first piece of ballet I ever witnessed—
trailing a chiffon shawl and tossing her dark hair
first over one shoulder, then the other.
The cousin from Syracuse looked away with set jaw,
and the other girls never left off their chattering,
but, empty cup raised to my lips, I couldn't take my eyes off her.
Every day after that, from my window or front walk,
I watched her amble past my house on the way to school,
loitering well behind the other children.
She must have always been late:
the bookbag in one hand and the lunch pail in the other
appeared to weigh her down as she zigzagged
down the street from sidewalk to sidewalk,
pausing whenever a bird or flower caught her eye.
Never once did she speak to me, or I to her.
And I was not invited back for another tea party,
even though—unlike her cousin, who had nodded off
    unhappily—
I thought I had played my part well,
repeatedly emptying my empty cup with gusto.
Then, in the spring, I stopped seeing her altogether,
no matter when I planted myself at the window.
I worked up the nerve to ask her sisters about her,
but without replying they brushed past me.
Other inquiries I made came to nothing.
Until just before my family moved away that summer
when suddenly everyone on Jupiter Place was talking
about her in lowered voices, with veiled expressions,
for in those days there was still a stigma attached
to anyone who contracted polio—another word
I had never heard before but would forever associate
with the name of that girl who had danced slowly

into the twilight beneath the darkening tree
even as her sisters cleared the table
and the rest of us were sent home.
A name I heard in a whisper twenty years later,
at the reenactment of an ancient festival on Rhodes,
when in the whirl of dancers moonlit in sheer robes
one collapsed by a precipice high over the sea;
a name I wanted to call out twenty years after that—
just today—as a woman on crutches passed me,
tossing her hair over her shoulder before disappearing
down the sidewalk, descending along the shadows
of the trees that ran like a ladder as far as I could see.
Kathryn.

Birds of Paradise in Ice Water

In this room where no one speaks above a whisper,
despite the absence of a sick or dying person
or the presence of anyone engaged
in a difficult or private task, a dozen
of the great flowers on their formidable stems
have been arranged in a glass pitcher before a picture
window looking down the long snow-covered street.

I have seen them growing wild by the hundreds
along a riverbank on a Pacific island.
As I dipped my oars silently so as not to frighten
birds from their perches, the flowers loomed suddenly,
the slashed-orange petals with their rainbow streaks
indeed like wings poised to take flight
through the curtain of mist descending the mountains.

The canopy on the glass building down the street
has frozen in place as the wind left it, curling upward,
like a wave cresting to break in the open sea,
and at the base of the vase what appeared to be clear stones
anchoring the stems are in fact ice cubes to keep the flowers
    crisp
as the day they were cut from steaming soil, under a fiery sky
in which hundreds of birds—brighter than fire—were wheeling.

Uncle Phillip's Funeral in Las Vegas

I.

No one came.
Bands of heat, like a rainbow, shimmered over the desert.
Two birds punctured a cactus with their beaks, drinking deeply.
A cloud the size of a silver dollar dissolved in the sun.
A woman in white, swinging her hips,
came out of the crematorium to meet the hearse.
She wore cherry lipstick and green mascara.
Her many bracelets clattered.
She introduced herself as the funeral director
and, smiling, swatted away a fly.

2.

He was a short, blustery man with blue eyes,
a barrel chest, and wavy white hair.
In his last days, putting away a fifth of Scotch daily
in a furnished studio overlooking a parking lot
in the Duke of Devon apartments,
he constructed a schooner inside a bottle,
which he left unfinished and labeled
"The Shipwreck in the Bottle."
This may have been his most inspired moment.

3.

At eighty-five, he smoked a corona every morning,
scanned the racing forms,
and watched the fights on television
with the sound turned off.

A man who in his youth had worked
as a stevedore and a bouncer,
who boxed for his supper in the makeshift rings
behind the stockyards on Lake Michigan,
he died in his sleep with a table fan ruffling the sheets.
Among his personal effects were a purple heart
awarded for valor in the Argonne forest in 1917,
an honorary badge from the Chicago Police Department,
a photograph of himself with Gene Tunney and Mayor Daley,
and the birth certificate of a daughter
(dated December 24, 1932, in Miami)
who died within a week, unnamed.

4.

None of his four wives survived him,
though the last was twenty years his junior,
and he had no other children.
In my childhood he sent me a hundred dollar bill
every Christmas, and once, on my birthday,
a pair of spats and an ebony walking stick.
Another year, there was a basket of mangoes
from San Juan and a telescope
with MONTE CARLO printed on the barrel.
When I was nine, summering at a house
in the mountains, he came to a family reunion,
arriving all the way from Detroit
in a chauffeur-driven Daimler with a box of kippers
(which he ate daily, for longevity),
a case of Johnnie Walker Black,
and a set of pool cues, though there was no pool table.
Also, one of his wives, a former showgirl
who sat on the front porch in a white dress
shooing away flies with a Japanese fan.

5.

His will, otherwise unremarkable, specified
that he be cremated at noon the day
after his death and that a recording of the Overture
to *Don Giovanni* be played in the chapel.
As the brief plume of smoke sailed into the sky
from the stack discreetly concealed by palms,
the funeral director sat alone in the rear,
oblivious to the music, and flipping open
her compact, inclining her head into the shadows,
applied lipstick to her parted lips.

Sleep

for Constance

In this blue room, behind salt-streaked shutters, you sleep,
the corner of the pillowcase beside your lips fluttering.
A spider is suspended from the ceiling fan,
and on the beach storm winds are lashing the breakers.

Today a cluster of black birds alighted, squawking, in a tree
dotted with red flowers beneath which I was sleeping.

Close by, the waves were sliding in through sheets of light,
and in the clouds a blue room appeared, identical to this room
in which I wind my way to sleep each night watching that spider
   spin.

Over the coast of this island, far from any continent, Antares,
the red star at the heart of Scorpio, is glowing brightly.

At dawn you will tell me how you saw that star from out at
   sea,
like a drop of blood in the night sky, as you tried to steady
your tossing skiff and return to shore, where loud birds
filled a solitary tree beside which I stood, waving you in.

On a Clear Night

In the Kyi Valley of Tibet, a snow-white desert
where an orchestra of lamas performs by starlight for the gods,
it is said that when we near death, and may least suspect it,
sorcerers disguised as people in our daily lives—
neighbors, postmen, shopkeepers—
steal a single breath from us, slip it into a bag,
and at the moment we expire deposit it
high in the mountains that hold up the sky.

Sometimes the sorcerers can assume the form
of someone even closer to us, a friend or relative,
or a lover opening her handbag on a street corner.
As you are doing now—while the strains
of an orchestra waft from a car radio—
rummaging for your comb, running it through your hair,
and then snapping the bag shut with a smile.
Taking my breath away.

Suicide Watch

In a sea of shadows
a building of locked windows
in which each light burns with the same low intensity
a man in a room without doors
is watching television and being watched
on a monitor in the next room

Beside him the paper flowers are wilting
bleached the same pale blue
as his paper slippers and the flimsy
robe he is wearing over thin
pajamas while sitting on a hard chair
his pockets stuffed with packs of gum

On the dark window images are reflected
off the television screen
two cars careering down a mountain road
a woman on a railway platform swooning
into the backdraft of a passing express
a mouse in a cartoon snatching cheese from a mousetrap

Then the screen goes blank and reflects only
the man rigidly poised with the lamps
dimming and all the light in the room
flowing into him so that he shines
stretching his arms out with upturned wrists
in a sea of shadows

A Visitor

Who are you and what do you want here?
Upon your arrival, birds swooped into the trees,
dogs cowered in the bushes,
and the one cat stepped through her own shadow
on a wall and disappeared.

Because you could only have come from one direction—
across the lake that is not yet frozen—
some concealed their fear of you better than others.
Many took flight, strewing the road with their possessions.
Others emerged to offer you gifts, in vain,

while praying you would not carry them away,
across the lake and the forest
to the icy mountains by the sea
where you began the long journey that has left
your eyes, hands, and stomach empty.

Now, instead of hair, black water is flowing
from your head, threatening to flood the fields,
to drown even the swiftest among us.
And still we'll have nothing to give you.
Not even a name.

The Creation of the Night Sky

Behind the rising curtains of mist
a small man in a long coat is riding a bicycle
along a cliff: though he can't reach
the pedals, he keeps picking up speed.
Breakers are crashing on the reefs.
A girl wearing goat bells on her ankles turns cartwheels.
In a stone building in bare cells
naked old men are sipping tea through straws.

If there is a city in heaven,
if there is a heaven, one of them thinks,
its music must be played on pianos clear as ice,
tinkling across space, never reaching a human ear.

At high tide the plants swell and the sand
darkens from below, like a bruise.
On the horizon umbrella-shaped clouds are opening.
Then the rain passes: dark lines on a diagonal, lightly smudged.
A bicycle without a rider is negotiating
the winding trail down the mountain.
And in the silence expansive as the seafloor
the stars light up, singly at first, then all at once, blazing.

From ATOMIC FIELD: TWO POEMS (2000)

from 1962

A girl is dyeing her bathing suit blue in a tub of hot water.
Her dog named Mambo is watching her.
The suit was originally white.
Mambo is white, with black spots on his head.
The girl says her mother, the widow, does the mambo
in their living room on Friday nights.
Sometimes with a man.
The next time I see the girl she tells me
that when she wore the bathing suit to the beach,
all the dye came out in the blue water.
Then she lifts her skirt to show me,
and her suit is white again, all right,
above her thin, suntanned legs.

There is always someone on crutches in this luncheonette.
Or so it seems.
A former GI.
A bus driver who was hit by a truck.
A nurse who never recovered from polio.
And behind the counter, the bald man
with the hook for a hand,
who can twirl his mustache with it.

At the bus stop a blind man sells colored pencils.
Ballpoint pens, too, at Thanksgiving and Christmas.
Ten cents for a pencil, two bits for a pen.
Around the corner, a boy from the orphanage
gives a bookmark to anyone who drops money into his box—
no matter if it's a nickel or a dollar.
A different boy every day, rotating by the month.
There are that many boys at the orphanage, I am told,
and I am grateful not to be one and fearful that I could be—
these boys in their coarse blue suits and thick-soled black shoes,
faces alternately fierce and frightened
and in their eyes the sad lights of distant ports
faintly flickering as they repeat the same refrain:
Alms for Saint Gregory,
the name of their orphanage,
the patron saint of shipwrecked sailors,
of lost travelers.

#22

At P.S. 28:
girls with budding breasts in Girl Scout uniforms;
classmates arm wrestling for quarters;
teachers (all women) smoking and applying makeup in their
    lounge;
a principal who sprinkles her speeches with Latin words;
a janitor with a red toupee
and a one-armed gym coach.
This is the place where I learn to read;
to give and take a punch in the playground;
to lie when absolutely necessary;
to multiply and divide;
to switch-hit a baseball;
to recite a poem by heart before an audience.
The poem is "Trees" by Joyce Kilmer
(the only work of his I will ever encounter)
and with it I conclude the tree-planting ceremony
in honor of a student who died of cancer.
Why I am chosen to play this role I don't know.
But that night I write my own version of the poem—
which I show no one—only to discover
with astonishment and secret delight
that I prefer it to the original.

Six doors down, a beautiful young woman
with golden hair lives alone in a yellow house.
She always dresses in yellow and gold
and wears heels, gloves, and amber glasses year round.
I don't know her name.
Working nights, coming home at dawn,
she is the subject of endless unflattering
speculation among the neighbors.
I think she might be a magician's assistant,
or one of the Rockettes.
She drives a two-tone Triumph—mustard & ocher—
touching the dashboard lighter to the cigarette
between her lips whenever she speeds around the corner.
Only after she isn't seen for a week
do we discover that she was a night court stenographer
who disappeared without a trace one morning.
Eventually her house is sold.
The new owner paints it white,
but to his surprise finds that no matter
what color tulips and roses he plants in the garden,
they always come up yellow, as do
the cherry tomatoes on their tangled vines.
And that after a solitary yellow canary
builds a nest in the one tree in the yard,
the apples sprouting on its branches shine gold—
a marvel, seeing that it isn't an apple tree at all.

In my most recurring nightmare
a wolf with a broken leg is trapped
with me in a freight elevator.
We're plunging down a shaftway flashing with green lights.
The wolf is snarling.
I keep circling away from him,
but he's cutting off the angle on me.
Closing in.
His leg is caked with blood.
His rolling eyes are white.
Finally we're falling so fast I can barely breathe
and the wolf rises up on his one good leg,
bows, and pulls from his throat
first my best friend
and then my friend's dog,
and though they're both dead
the dog is barking
and my friend is shouting at me,
"Jump—jump!"
But there's nowhere to jump from,
and nothing to jump to.

Successive snowstorms have lined the streets
with bands of ice, like sedimentary stone.
While his wife is being fitted for fur-lined boots,
the undertaker is holding forth in the shoe store
about the fine points of burial in frozen ground,
edifying the clerk, who's looking up the wife's skirt.
The undertaker has the tidiest, tightest garden on our street,
maintained by moonlighting workmen from the cemetery.
He himself never puts a spade to earth at home.
He spends his free time in the garage,
regularly steaming clean the components of his car engine,
then reassembling it—the V-8 from a 1950 Cadillac sedan,
black as coal, that runs so quietly
you can't hear it, even on the stillest night.

With a shard of ice I scratch my name
on the surface of the frozen lake:
as ice cuts into ice, can a diamond
(which leaves its mark on all things)
scratch another diamond?
And if so, is it the more valuable diamond
that prevails, or the industrial variety?
No such question arises with ice,
which any way you cut it, is H_2O;
my name's engraved on it,
and though it may be covered by snow
and worn down by wind,
will remain so until the lake thaws,
returning to that blackness with which I was one
before I ever had a name.

The flesh the flesh-eating plants eat
turns out to be houseflies and ants
which the librarian daily introduces
through sliding panels in the terraria
that sit beneath a tall window in the lobby
where the motes of dust perpetually spin:
the Cobra Plant, the Sundew, the Yellow Pitcher,
and of course the Venus Flytrap *(Dionaea muscipula)*
whose flowers themselves are fleshlike, waxy.
This is a common characteristic among the members
of the *Droseraceae* family,
which also are noted for
their tufts of hair and bloodlike sap.
A neatly typed sign on the wall
adds that there are larger varieties
in South America capable of entrapping
birds and rodents, and in Malaysia
a colony of the *Nepenthes* family
which is rumored to thrive on wild goats
and the occasional human being,
and that for obvious reasons
none of these plants will be exhibited any time soon.
In front of the library
the hot dog vendor smears mustard, relish, and onions
on his twenty-five-cent special
which it is pleasant to eat slowly,
sitting in the sun on the granite steps
and watching the cars go by.

On the 27th of October I am told to say my prayers.
On television entire congregations in cathedrals
are shown to be on their knees, clutching candles and praying.
In Cuba, ninety miles from Florida,
nuclear missiles are directed at American cities,
first and foremost New York
where I too light a candle and go to my knees
beside my bed for only the second time in my life to pray
that I will reach my twelfth birthday, in February,
and that the president will see his way through the darkness
to a place where none of us will have to die.
The first time I prayed like this was on the night
last year when my grandfather was dying.
And he died soon afterward.
(The next time will be a year from now,
on the day the president is shot,
and he too will die soon afterward.)
But tonight I fall asleep reviewing the route
I will follow to the nearest fallout shelter,
at the Masonic lodge,
and the posture I will assume—
knees tucked up, head buried in my arms—
when a wall of fire topples the city like a toy,
only to wake to the news that the crisis has ended,
the missiles are being shipped back to Russia.
We're safe again.

#40

When my friend casts his line by moonlight,
the fish stream to it.
Night fishing is his specialty.
Making his way downstream by zigzagging
over the many footbridges that span the still pools
where the trout hover, quicker than shadows.
Returning home just before dawn
with his basket full of fish
and sometimes too the pockets of his jeans
and the even deeper pockets of his worn corduroy jacket
with the bloodstains on the sleeves
and the smell so strong
that I pick it up long before I see or hear him
down the street with his rod over his shoulder
when he comes to dig for worms
under the pachysandra in my yard.
The fish trust that smell, he tells me,
that's why they come to me.

In pointy shoes that lace up the sides—twist shoes—
and pancho shirts that don't tuck in
people are doing the twist.
Round and round and up and down . . .
That's Chubby Checker in his signature black suit
and patent leather twist shoes
twisting on the Ed Sullivan Show.
And Joey Dee and the Starlighters at a row of mikes
under pink spotlights
at the Peppermint Lounge
way over on the West Side
where the line of people waiting to get in,
their coats and hats white with snow,
stretches for four blocks.
And the name of the dance is the "Peppermint Twist" . . .
On the radio you can hear the twist night and day.
At the school dance no other dance is danced.
Everybody's doing it,
come on, baby, and do the twist.
In the auditorium one day, drifting off collectively into a
    golden haze,
we're told the times are complex by a visiting psychologist.
That no point is reached by way of a straight line.
And no one can insist anymore that he alone knows
right from wrong, and then enforce that knowledge.
Not with the specter of the mushroom cloud hovering.
I notice that even the psychologist is wearing twist shoes.
Round and round and up and down . . .

In a house outlined by Christmas lights,
where wreaths hang in the windows
and plastic reindeer are spotlighted on the lawn,
girls in long nightgowns, like ghosts,
stand before mirrors and comb out their hair,
hundreds of brushstrokes into the night.
I'm a houseguest, sitting by the fire,
when one of them lets me in on her recurring dream:
an alpine plateau dotted with crosses,
beneath glass peaks,
where she's a climber caught in an avalanche.
And every time I dream it, she says,
another hair on my head turns white.

#1

On New Year's Eve,
having dropped five hundred mikes of acid at ten-thirty
in order to feel the first rushes at midnight,
we turn the stereo up,
place the speakers in the window facing outward,
and recline on the Indian carpet
with the burgundy and orange renderings of Vishnu and
    Lakshmi
locked in coitus,
the sun blazing on his forehead,
the moon on hers.
And locked together ourselves,
the carpet now streaming thousands of colors
into an arc that spans the room,
a rainbow of electrical impulses
beneath which we are protected forever
from the forces of the night,
the darkness pressing into this building
at the center of the city,
we suddenly hear beating wings approaching
and realize it is Vayu, the god of wind,
ruler of the fallen realms,
who is streaking across the sea,
beneath blue clouds,
to carry off everyone but us.
For at dawn, it's true, we're still here,
shivering on the floor of this empty room
where the steam pipes knock and hiss
but produce no heat.

A room illuminated by the rays of black crystals
arranged in a circle on the lacquered table.
Beside them, a checkered cloth with talismans
we can move from square to square
while behind the curtain an invisible woman,
plucking a single note on a Japanese harp,
divines the future.
In the corner, the wick of a red candle flames to life.
A clock strikes six o'clock.
And none of us sitting around this table—
itself a revolving circle within the square room—
know if it's morning or evening.
To which someone remarks, Why should it matter?
And all the while the moon is rising full
between the thin buildings,
its mountains and seas icily clear,
easily mapped—unlike the landscapes
we're roaming in our heads,
the vast, inked-in expanses
where everything is possible and nothing changes.

In the waiting room a woman
in a Salvation Army coat and scuffed boots
who has accompanied her sister
is sipping weak coffee from a Styrofoam cup
and staring down a dark linoleum corridor
when she tells me she read somewhere
that in a single second 1.2 million people
around the world arrive and depart
in railroad terminals and airports,
at bus stops, taxi queues, and ferry slips.
"Everything is in motion and every place is a station," she adds,
"even this place."
Neither of us says another word
before the man who was once a doctor
in his pale green gown and horn-rimmed glasses
comes through the door expressionless
and nods to me that it's over with the woman
I accompanied there in the predawn, who was,
and is no longer, two months pregnant by my friend.
He is in jail for hurling blood
onto the windows of the recruiting center
to protest the war.
And now his girlfriend and the doctor have broken
the law, with me a silent witness,
an accomplice, but not yet
a criminal myself as far as I know.

When she comes off her shift at the VA hospital
where she tends the recent arrivals from Vietnam,
the amputees and paraplegics
and the shell-shocked boys,
some of them younger than me,
who often wake, she tells me,
feeling pain in their missing limbs,
we rendezvous near the boathouse,
watching the scullers fly by,
or at the old cemetery
on a cement bench
hidden among the hawthorn bushes.
She's still in uniform,
white stockings, shoes, and the dress
that I unbutton just far enough
to slip my hand in over her breasts
when we start to kiss
there in the sun,
and she always touches
my legs and my arms
one by one before embracing me fully
as the wind picks up off the river
and carries the scents of the flowers
that grow wild on its banks.

#9

The pulse I feel behind my knees,
in my groin,
at the base of my skull
is echoed in the music you're playing,
broadcast from other galaxies
and picked up by radio telescopes.
Those stars are so cold and faraway
and you're so close and warm,
opening your arms,
your mouth,
and in the next breath your legs
under this rough woolen blanket
with the mazelike pattern—
a map of the Apache spirit world—
on the cabin's pine floor.
One day you'll be as faraway
as those stars—
no, farther—
and sending back no music.

Sleeping in a cold room on the rue de Rennes,
counting the stars through the icy skylight,
steeping oolong tea and boiling fusilli on the wood stove.
Everything carefully accounted for:
wood: 40 francs a cord;
tea: 20 francs for 4 ounces;
fusilli: 30 francs a kilo.
The real heat,
under a purple quilt from the Arab quarter,
is provided by your body,
which unknown to us,
is already being eaten away by the cancer
that will kill you before the year is out.
Your funeral plot in Vevey: 2,000 francs.
In the room off this room where you work
you'll leave behind a set of lithographs:
Arctic landscapes in silver light.
I remember the day you began them.
Your blonde hair flying by the river.
The children in pale blue robes begging for alms.
The plane trees blackening at dawn.
And those stars through the skylight:
the brightest of them no star at all,
but Venus, never flickering,
that forever after will rule my life.

We're on a mountain overlooking Spain that can only be
   climbed from France.
In one of those countries that is not really a country, called
   Andorra.
Stones white as skulls dot the stream flickering behind the
   trees.
The same stones from which this farmhouse was built long ago.
The wine in the cellar, from Morocco, is black in a black
   bottle,
on its label a cluster of stars on a circular vine—
like Ariadne's corona, glittering among the constellations.
In the fireplace we crisscross planks from the burned-down
   barn
while blown snow, fine as sand, glazes the windows.
When I cut the loaf of bread we brought from the village,
I find a gold coin, neither Spanish nor French,
on which a woman with outspread wings
and flying hair is perched on a moonlit peak.
A coin which the following evening in town purchases us
a sumptuous dinner and a choice room at the tiny hotel
where the proprietor says we may remain as long as we like,
so rare is that coin, minted in Andorra itself—
a country with no mint and no currency of its own.

#23

The rain crossing the tarred rooftops stops suddenly.
The wine I'm drinking is bright yellow,
centered with white lights.
The bread you're breaking is veined like marble,
gold and white.
A man comes to the door.
Then a woman.
We hear tambourines, a mandolin, a taut drum down the
    steep stairwell.
All night they accompany the dancers.
There is a doctor on the Bergenstrasse
who will sell us opium crystals.
His nurse wears a green dress and black stockings.
She is always on the telephone,
peering through the venetian blinds at the arcade
where old men in children's clothes line up
to shoot pellet guns at metal ducks.
This accounts for the truckload of stuffed animals at the
    corner.
Now it's afternoon again.
The water in the water pipes in this building has turned to
    blood.
The windows are barred with sunlight—stronger than steel.
Color me black.
White.
Gold.
And cover me.
I'm cold.

The nightclub lies in a labyrinth of tunnels
beneath the rain-swept streets.
Beginning at midnight, the acts are:
a one-armed clown who plays the violin,
a stripper with three breasts,
a pair of talking dogs that converse in Chinese,
and—the finale—an androgynous couple
done up as mermaid and merman
who copulate underwater in a glass tank.
At the bar, under green lights, a line of men
in identical green suits stare into martini glasses
that widen every hour, like whirlpools.
The bartender's black glasses reflect everything
many times—like an insect's eye.
The waitresses are multiarmed, like Shiva,
and some of them have wings.
And then there's the band:
bass, drums, piano, and clarinet,
to which the clown adds his violin
and one of the dogs the castanets
as they become a sextet
and play without interruption until dawn,
when the bouncer, blinking, with blood-stained knuckles,
coughs into his sleeve
and all the lights come up—
slowly, like the sun.

As the sun gilds the Arno and shades the stern faces
of the angels atop the cathedral,
two busses collide, toppling a statue of Machiavelli,
fire sweeps a school for the blind,
a nun finds an apple ripening on a pear tree.
At my hotel an old woman is crossing the lobby
in a shimmering dress
with a parrot on her shoulder
who is said to possess knowledge
of stars not yet born,
dreams not yet dreamed
crimes not yet committed.
After the hills darken and the torn clouds scatter,
the parrot ascends to a palm tree
in the mezzanine and begins squawking
names, dates, places—
his particular secret history of the living and the dead
that may never come to pass.

A church filled with fiery flowers,
with widows in white and brides in black, milling.
At the midpoint of this broiling summer,
as waves of napalm crest in jungles
on the other side of the world
where every second someone is dying for nothing
while someone else is being sacrificed
in the name of something larger than himself,
I'm an island on an island
of two thousand living people
and five millennia of diaphanous souls
who have journeyed beyond the sun to become
(according to Hipparchus, himself born here)
stars, each of them, on the sphere that encloses
all things, including this girl dancing
along the seawall with bloodied feet,
trailing a fishnet delicate as lace,
the flame of her hair fanned by the wind
and her eyes bright as the candles
the mourners carry through the town at night,
every night,
down the same sequence of alleys
to the sea.

On the southern coast of Crete
where even the shadows of the palms smolder
and tumblers of raki waft smoke
and steam pours from bursting melons,
naked girls are lolling, burnt-orange, in the boiling surf.
They live in the black caves along the beach,
and for a week I'm one of their guests,
drinking wine mixed with honey,
making love between handwoven blankets,
gazing cross-legged at the thin line
that is Africa shimmering on the horizon.
Some Americans in loincloths have founded
a school of Pythagoras in a hut beneath the cliffs.
They eat only figs, olives, and barley cakes
and at nightfall play lutes and timbrels
and watch stars across the galaxy conjoin into circles
which mesh like the gears of a clock,
measuring—to the last second—every man's life.

Today while snow slants into Manhattan,
the black and white flakes
like sparks off a flint,
two men step onto the moon.
Their footprints will remain in the deep dust
long after the last man has walked the earth.
While icicles bar the window
and snakes hiss in the radiators,
I remain in your bed all day, jet-lagged,
a cashmere blanket pulled to my chin
until you return from work,
unzip your dress,
unfasten your bra,
peel off your stockings
and slide in beside me with the cold
scent of the wind in your hair.
While the astronauts who left Florida
three days ago wander the airless valley
of Taurus-Littrow on the moon's equator,
my mouth finds yours,
your breath fills my lungs,
the blue of your eyes spills over like water.
From the earth, the moon glows white;
from the moon, the earth is starkly lit;
but at 3 A.M. when you cross the room naked,
it's your body that shines so bright.

The books are piled high in the corners:
Blake, Céline, Bulgakov, Kleist,
Li Po and Jarry,
Suetonius and Procopius,
and the complete works of Fyodor Mikhailovich Dostoevski.
The ashtrays are overflowing.
A candle stuck in an empty vodka bottle is burning at noon.
A photograph of Wild Bill Hickok has been blown up, wall-size.
Let It Bleed is playing on the phonograph
with four LPs stacked above it.
In the soup pot on the stove carrots and potatoes
are tumbling in boiling water.
The telephone is ringing in another room.
The doorbell is ringing in another life.
Who will come through that door,
across time and space,
defying laws of life and death,
to deliver a message.
Something like: *You think you're here, but you're not here.*
Or: *Years from now you'll try to imagine*
this instant and yourself so lost in it.
Or maybe yourself just oblivious:
to the express trains racing through the night
with their upright passengers masquerading as the dead;
to the sun's myriad satellites reflecting its rays;
to the snatch of dialogue, from a dream, which someone
    scrawled
on the bathroom mirror with purple lipstick.
Yes, who was it who did that?

Trucks are salting the streets.
The airports have closed.
In this long empty room the shadow
of a lemon tree flutters on the wall.
The last record played hours ago,
but the stereo's lights,
like rubies and emeralds,
continue to flicker.
The blanket on the bed is paper-thin,
the pillow is like stone.
I was dreaming of myself
in such a bed
drawing a map that encompassed
all the cities I just passed through—
Paris Trieste Athens Ravenna—
except that it resembled a map
of the Amazonian jungle,
vast forests and countless tributaries
off a serpentine river.
Until I wake up, I feel certain
this map could have guided me around Europe,
or anywhere else I chose to go.
Meanwhile, through the frozen window,
an ocean liner, white as an iceberg,
is sailing down the Hudson
for the open sea.

From my corner table beneath a blue light
the palms are swaying,
the drummer's steel brushes slide
across his ride cymbal like an ocean wave.
A woman wearing a black dress
imprinted with white roses
downs a tumbler of blue liquor,
closes her eyes, and finds herself
transported to a velodrome
banked like the rings of Saturn.
Closing my eyes, I travel more modestly,
to the recent memory of Saint Nicholas
eyeing me severely from the wall panel
of a chapel on the island of Poros,
where the streets are whitewashed daily.
Here on Manhattan Island it takes a blizzard
to whitewash the streets,
and the gods who reveal themselves to us
are famously pitiless, cold, and rife with knowledge.
Walled in by bricks of ice,
illuminated by a guttering candle,
you (or someone impersonating you)
begin explaining the mechanics of salvation
before preceding me into the snow,
the wind that rattles our bones like sticks,
the night like a vast tide that carries all things away.

#45

Tomorrow, the New Year, the world begins anew.
Or so they say.
Some will depart this place.
Others will remain.
A few will count themselves lucky.
Many will be unlucky.
Just before midnight, I drift away
from my third party in as many hours
and find myself in a darkened room
overlooking the park, the swaying treetops
laden with snow beneath a rising moon.
It was once thought the souls
of the dead resided on the moon,
in glass buildings like this one,
and, for diversion, gazed to earth,
at the wars, famines, and migrations,
the floods and fires that destroyed whole cities.
The Apollo astronauts who just walked on the moon
will be the last men to do so in this century.
When one of them visited Nepal soon afterward,
children lined the mountain roads with candles
and bowed to him as they would to a god.
Tonight if there are gods looking down at us,
at our own follies and disasters,
will they continue merely to order our fates
(even as we resolve to change them),
or will they embrace us at last
in all their splendor, and set us free?